# CLERGY
# TALES

## — TAILS —

# CLERGY TALES

## — TAILS —

Volumes:

1:  Who Wags the Dog?
2.  Wagging: Friendly but Exhausting
3.  When God Wags the Tale

STEPHEN McCUTCHAN

www.smccutchan.com

PRIMIX
PUBLISHING
THE WRITE CHOICE

Primix Publishing
11620 Wilshire Blvd
Suite 900, West Wilshire Center, Los Angeles, CA, 90025
www.primixpublishing.com
Phone: 1-800-538-5788

This is a work of fiction. Names, characters, places, and incidents are a product of the author's imagination. Locales and public names are sometimes used for atmospheric purposes. Any resemblance to actual people, living or dead, or to businesses, companies, events, institutions, or locales is completely coincidental.

Scripture quotes are from NRSV unless otherwise noted.

Published by Primix Publishing: 03/11/2024

ISBN: 979-8-89194-099-4(sc)
ISBN: 979-8-89194-101-4(e)

Library of Congress Control Number: 2024901845

Any people depicted in stock imagery provided by iStock are models, and such images are being used for illustrative purposes only.

Certain stock imagery © iStock.

Because of the dynamic nature of the Internet, any web addresses or links contained in this book may have changed since publication and may no longer be valid. The views expressed in this work are solely those of the author and do not necessarily reflect the views of the publisher, and the publisher hereby disclaims any responsibility for them.

# CONTENTS

*This book is dedicated to my wife*
*Sandra Jo Bowman McCutchan*
*who has supported, nurtured, and encouraged me*
*through my living through similar tales of ministry.*

# CALLED BY GOD

*When in doubt my steps*
*Begin to slow*
*And I question what I do*
*Or what I know*
*Then from heaven I sense a smile*
*And a chuckle from eternity all the while*
*As a word or act interrupts my space*
*With just the needed glimpse of grace*

Stephen McCutchan

# 1

## YOUR BROTHER'S BLOOD
## IS CRYING OUT

Al Chippingham lowered his six-foot-one-inch, slightly overweight frame into a chair at Konkles, his favorite coffee house. He felt the pain of his new resolve to begin working out at the gym. Sports had never been his passion, but he recognized that he was nearing 40 and needed to pay attention to his weight. He reached for a napkin and began to clean his trifocal glasses. He chided himself for feeling both nervous and excited at being here this morning.

A couple of weeks ago, he received an email from a seminary classmate with whom he had lost touch with but had never forgotten. He thought about his relationship with Carla Espinosa. She was a fiery Latina, one of the few Hispanics in the seminary. Her slim figure, olive-toned complexion, and jet-black hair immediately caught people's attention, but her in-your-face, no-injustice-should-be-ignored, and no-barrier-too-high approach to life frightened most people, including Al. In contrast, he was shy and gangly and found refuge in books and ideas. His debates were with professors and not frontline protests.

Yet, for some reason still a mystery to him, the two found a camaraderie that transcended their differences. It was not a romantic relationship but rather a respectful exchange of ideas that both found stimulating. Well, Al thought, I guess we did have one date—sort of. They were both in a class that focused on social issues. As they were discussing the issue of race and discrimination, someone spoke of a scene from *Gone With the Wind.* Both Al and Carla admitted that they had never seen the movie. Near the end of their final semester, Al noticed that the movie was being shown in a classic film series in a nearby community. They decided to go together.

That was nine years ago. They graduated, said friendly goodbyes, promised to keep in touch, and went their separate ways. A couple of years ago, he remembered seeing an article in the newspaper on immigration and border crossings. Right in the middle of the article was a picture of five-foot-two-inch Carla standing toe-to-toe with a beefy six-foot-four-inch border guard arguing her case. He had chuckled at the time and thought to himself, *Carla has not changed a bit.* He wanted to get in touch but felt that would be intrusive, so he just admired her courage from afar.

Two weeks ago, an email arrived. Carla was invited to address a meeting of his presbytery about her Hispanic ministry. She wondered if they could get together for coffee, catch up on old times, and discuss the best approach for her presentation to this regional body of Presbyterian churches. He gave her directions to Konkles Coffee House and suggested that they meet at 10 a.m.

He arrived early to make sure they had a table. Early in his ministry, he learned that being honest about how he was feeling gave him greater control of his actions and response. Now, as he waited, he turned to that habit. He chided himself a little for feeling both anxious and excited. Al's only serious adult relationship with a woman had been a disaster. It ended with a fair amount of pain. It confirmed for Al that he was not very skilled in intimate relationships.

He recalled an old cartoon where Charlie Brown said plaintively, "I love humanity; it's people I can't stand." The reverse was normally true for Al. Sometimes he looked on humanity with feelings of despair, but he loved the people who made up his congregations. So, Al thought, I'd have to amend that statement slightly. I love people, but an intimate relationship with a single woman scares the hell out of me. Now he was meeting with the beautiful Carla Espinosa, who he had never dared to think of as more than a fun friendship. Lord, if she can just come in with about fifty more pounds, a macho husband with tattoos, and perhaps three bratty children, I think I will be able to comport myself quite well.

Then he saw her marching through the door as if she owned the place. Her lustrous hair flowed over her shoulders, her dark eyes flashed, and the blue jeans and light blue work shirt neither displayed nor hid an unwanted ounce. He wished he'd started working out several months ago and given in to the temptation of getting contact lenses. He felt a stupid grin come over his face as he rose to indicate where he was sitting.

Her bright teeth sparkled in a warm smile as she quickened her pace, opened her arms, and enveloped him in a warm embrace. "Que bueno," she said. "It is so good to see you after all these years. You look wonderful."

It pleased him to see a number of people in the room take notice of this greeting. He might not know what to do next, but at least it was a great beginning.

One of the shaggy-haired waiters arrived immediately and asked how he could serve them. They ordered a dark-roasted Columbian coffee and bagels. Then, like teenagers returning after a summer at the beach, they launched into sharing stories and recalling fond memories from their seminary experience. When the coffee and bagels arrived, Carla carefully added the cream cheese as Al watched her. He noticed that she did not have a ring on her finger but decided that was not a proper subject for inquiry—yet.

Carla grew quiet as she took a bite of her bagel and visibly began to relax. "What a unique hideaway," she said as she looked around. "I'm glad you chose it. Sitting here, you could almost forget the world outside existed."

Al's skills of ministry included a sixth sense of reading unexpressed emotions. He looked more closely. He noticed some lines of pain around her eyes and a slight tremor in her hand as she lifted her cup of coffee. "Carla, it's been a long time since we've talked, but I remember that you were never very good at being politely cheerful when you were feeling deeply about something. Enough of the fun catching up— what's going on for you?"

She looked up, eyes glistening, but chose to take another bite of bagel and chew it slowly before she spoke. "Madre de Dios, you are good. I'll bet you are a fantastic pastor, Al. I think I need a pastor now. Can you be my pastor for the next couple of hours and help me pull myself together?"

"The pastor side of me knows," said Al, "that I should now say in a dispassionate and calming voice, 'Tell me more about what is bothering you.' The friend side is almost afraid to hear about the pain that I sense in you."

"I know it's selfish of me to lay this on you after we haven't been in contact for so many years, but I need both sides of you this morning." She reached out and shoved his plate with the bagel on it toward him. "You may want to get some nourishment first."

"Actually," Al said, "I'm trying to lose weight. Go ahead and tell me what's going on."

"Do you know what my ministry is?" Carla asked.

"I know it has something to do with the border ministry and the issue of people trying to cross into this country," said Al. "I remember seeing a picture of you in the paper a couple of years ago facing down a border guard. He must have outweighed you by a hundred pounds, but you didn't seem to give an inch."

"There was a picture of that in the papers?" she laughed. "I hope the caption was something like "Un Tigre taking a bite for libertad." The chance to laugh seemed to smooth some of the pain lines in her face.

"Facing down officials must really be draining. The law is supposed to protect people, not be part of the problem," Al said.

"In many ways the law and its officials are good. Many of the border guards are just decent people trying to keep order in society," Carla said. "It's just that sometimes you realize there is something greater than the law at stake."

I have trouble imagining the challenges you face, said Al.

When I emailed you a couple of weeks ago, I mainly wanted some advice about how to approach the meeting at your presbytery. I still want to talk about that. However, a couple of days ago, I had an experience that so unnerved me—I worry about my ability to keep my composure at the meeting.

I have the time," said Al, "and as both pastor and friend, I want you to tell me what happened."

"Most of these people who try to cross the borders are desperate for a better way of life," Carla began. "I know what the U.S. laws are, but a major part of my ministry is caring for these people in any way that I can. Usually it's just a drink of water here, some first aid there. . ." Then she began to tremble just slightly but enough that she had to stop and take a couple of deep breaths.

"What happened a couple of days ago?" Al asked and then waited until she could respond.

"We arrived too late. That's what happened. A mother along with her infant daughter had just died. She had given her share of water to her teenage son so that he might live. She was desperate for her family to have a chance at a new life and risked everything. She scraped together $5,000 to pay a coyote to lead them across the desert, and the SOB abandoned them half way across." Carla bit her lip to keep from crying.

"I'm sorry, Carla," Al said. "That is horrible."

"I may not be smart enough to solve the immigration problem in this country, but I am quite certain that my God, who is not restricted by all of these lines that humans have drawn, does not want that to happen to a mother and her children."

The coffee had grown cold during their conversation. They didn't seem to notice.

Al reached across the table and touched her hand. "We haven't had much contact since seminary, but I've always seen you as a friend in ministry. It hurts to see you in this much pain."

"Thanks. I'll be all right. It just hurts to see people suffer when all they want is to have a decent life. It's just not right."

"This is the pastor speaking, Carla. Stay in touch with that anger and tell me with whom you are angry. Is it the one you call a coyote, the border guards, God, who?"

"I'd like to kill that coyote with my bare hands. No, better, I would like to castrate him with a rusty knife, really slow, and watch him scream in horror." She brushed her hand as if swatting a fly. "But he's such an insignificant insecto, he doesn't even deserve to be squashed. No, what I'm really angry about is how easily most of the world just ignores the suffering as if they weren't important."

As if to reinforce what she was saying, some laughter burst forth from another table, and two people rose to give each other a high five. Both Al and Carla looked over at them and then back at each other.

"I wish I had a decent answer for that, Carla. Not at the depth that you have described, but in some ways, as a pastor, I see people's capacity to shield themselves from other people's pain all the time. To be honest, I do that myself sometimes."

"I don't expect an answer," said Carla. "I just need to share with someone I can trust. What do you expect will happen at the presbytery meeting?"

"To be honest," Al grimaced, "I think they will admire your courage, be touched by your stories, and be afraid to take any significant action that might upset the people in their congregations."

Carla threw up her hands as if to defend herself. "You don't have to pull your punches, Al. Go ahead and tell me the whole truth."

"I guess I could have softened that a bit."

"No, Al, I've always known you as someone who speaks straight. I need to know what to expect."

"I'm sure that some will want to say that even though it is tragic, still they were breaking the law when they tried to cross the border."

"And they will be right. But the law they are breaking is a misdemeanor. People shouldn't die for a misdemeanor."

Carla glanced down at the table and noticed some initials carved into the table. She traced the carving with her finger and then looked up.

"Do you know that there are graveyards along the All American

Canal where people are just dumped without any identification? Their own families will never know what happened to them. They don't even have a table with their initials on it."

"It feels so far from my world," said Al. "I'm not even sure what I can do, let alone our presbytery."

One of our professors pointed out that it was a foreign lay person, not the religious leaders, who responded to the need of the one who fell among the robbers."

"I know it sounds defensive, but these pastors are not bad people, Carla. Most pastors I know genuinely want to be faithful and respond to human need, but they feel a lot of pressure to compromise when it comes to speaking out. How did you get to be so courageous?"

"I don't feel very brave, Al. Most of the time I'm scared, but I'm not sure I have any choice. It's like those unknown people are crying out to me from their graves."

"I'm not sure I understand."

"Did I ever tell you about how I came to understand God's call in my life?"

"Isn't it ironic?" Al said. "Seminarians spend three years in seminary preparing for the ministry, and I don't recall any conversation during that time about God's call in our lives. I guess you always seemed so focused, and I was so busy sorting out my own life that I never stopped to ask."

Carla looked up at the ceiling as if to compose her thoughts. "I wasn't always so focused. My father was a union organizer with Caesar Chavez."

"So that's where you got your interest in politics?"

"Yeah, it is in my blood, I guess. I went to the University of New Mexico with the assumption that I would become a lawyer. I didn't have the guts that my father had, but I thought maybe I could work behind the scenes and help out in some way."

"Carla, ever since I've known you, you've been on the front line of all the social justice issues. I would hardly say that you lacked courage. In fact, that always intimidated me when I was around you."

"You, intimidated? I always saw you as the guy with all the

answers. Did you ever get anything less than an A in any of your classes?"

"Grades came easy for me, but I always knew that I was just a scared little boy hiding behind my books. I was like the tin man in the Wizard of Oz."

Carla smiled. "I guess neither of us knew what was behind each other's curtain."

Al tasted the cold coffee in front of him and grimaced. "So how did it change for you?"

"I'm not so sure it changed. Maybe I got better at hiding behind the curtain. There was one event, however, that changed my direction. Do you know what the government agency ICE is?"

"It has something to do with immigration, doesn't it?"

"Yes," Carla said. "It stands for Immigration Customs Enforcement, but the acronym is very apt. Just the thought of ICE sends chills down the spine of every Latino living in this country, legal or not."

"So what happened?"

"Well, it wasn't a dark and stormy night," said Carla, "but it was a rather cloudy day on campus. I was in a sullen mood. I'd left my political science class and was walking across campus. A boy I sort of liked had just told me that I didn't figure into his future plans. I think I was more upset at being rejected than ending the relationship."

"He must have been blind," Al said.

Carla looked up and smiled as Al's face turned red.

"Thanks, but that wasn't the worst thing that happened that day. I heard sirens and saw three dark vans coming on campus. Some men in uniforms got out, and all of us knew that it was the ICE. "

"One of the male students went up to them and demanded to know what they were doing on campus. We always thought of campus as being sort of a sanctuary."

"What happened?"

"They threw him to the ground and cuffed him. Then they demanded to see his papers. These guys were acting first and worrying about what was legal later."

"So much for law and order," Al said.

"Laws are meant to preserve order for the Caucasian majority," Carla said. "For Latinos it's just the mechanism for harassing you and reminding you that you really don't belong here."

Al shifted in his chair. "I'd like to explore that further some other time, but right now I want you to finish your story."

"Well, big brave Carla ran. I knew that they would start demanding to see our papers, and none of us carried papers around on campus. I'm a citizen, but I knew that because I was a Mexican with dark skin, I'd be hassled like all the rest."

"Where did you run to?"

"That's what's so strange," Carla said. "I know that you met me in seminary, but back then I had rejected the church. I had concluded that the Catholic church was part of the problem in Mexico, and the Protestant churches either were after our money or so focused on the afterlife that they ignored the injustices around them. As far as I was concerned, God was irrelevant if He existed at all. And yes, God was a He. One more male that was oppressing women and using His followers to rip off the poor." Carla looked up with an embarrassed smile. "Sorry, the feelings are still there, I guess."

"For not believing that God existed, you were pretty angry at him," Al said.

"That occurred to me later, but at the time, I was just a scared little Latina who tried to find a place to hide. Guess where I went?"

"I was guessing the administration building, but that must be wrong."

"That would make sense because they could attest to my citizenship, but for reasons I can't explain, I ran to the chapel. I don't think I'd even been in the chapel since freshman orientation."

"Sounds to me like a chapter right out of the Hound of Heaven," Al said.

"I'm not sure I understand."

"It's an old poem by a man named Francis Thompson," Al said. "It probably was written in the early 1900's. Most people have never read the poem, but the image of God like a hound who patiently but persistently pursues the hare seems to stick with people. You studied the law. I'm told that the poem was actually the source of the phrase with all deliberate speed in the Supreme Court's 1954 decision about school desegregation."

"I'll have to read it. Anyway, I wasn't the only one in the chapel that day. The chaplain came in and saw a group of us there. Without any hesitation, he locked the door. When the ICE came, he shouted through the door that they had no authority in God's house, and they should go see the administration."

"Strong chaplain," Al said.

"It was weird. He was a short, bespectacled, pudgy little guy. I'd never talked to him. Around campus, he just seemed to exist—sort of a nonentity to me. Yet, on that day, when he spoke, those big tough guys hesitated. They tried to threaten him but he wouldn't back down."

"So they went away?"

"No, eventually we had to come out, but first they did go to the administration. After some protracted negotiations, it all worked out. Unfortunately, some people among us didn't have the proper papers. They were taken away."

Al got a puzzled look on his face. "That was when you had a sense of call from God?"

"Oh no. I'm a tough old hare." Carla made a motion with her hand like a rabbit running away. "However, that was the beginning of the process. What I saw that day were the limits of the law and academia and the strange power of faith. It was almost like God was saying to me, 'When all else fails, I've got your back.'"

"And that gave you your courage?" Al asked.

"No, that taught me when I was scared out of my skin, which I often am, I'm not alone. I was really scared when I came to seminary, but by then I wanted to know what this God thing was all about."

"I remember when I first saw you. You were standing toe-to-toe with the dean demanding that he look into the wages that the seminary was paying the cleaning crew. You looked so righteous, like a prophet from the Bible; I almost felt sorry for the dean."

Carla stood up. "I can't stand cold coffee." She refilled her coffee cup. When she was seated, she looked at Al and said, "I first noticed you in a New Testament class, arguing with the professor. You were citing different passages and referencing different Greek and Hebrew words. I thought you might be the smartest person I'd ever seen. I promised myself I would never get in an argument with you about anything biblical."

"Words are my best weapon. I always feel comfortable when it's an intellectual argument. How about that? Each of us were intimidated by the other right off the bat. How did we get to be friends?"

"Cautiously, I think," Carla said. "Though I was impressed with the fact that you always treated me kindly and with respect. You didn't seem threatened by the fact that I was a woman, which is more than I can say for some of our other male classmates, and yet, you didn't hesitate to challenge me when you didn't agree."

"So what finally tipped the scales and brought you to seminary?" Al pressed.

"I think," said Carla, "it was the stories that my dad used to tell me about Caesar Chavez and how centered he was in his faith. I wanted that type of courage, and if faith could get me there, then I wanted to give it a try." She sat up straighter and said, "Hey, I've bared my soul to you, now it's your turn. Did you always know that God was calling you?"

"I'm afraid my story is not as dramatic as yours," Al said.

"So God is a versatile hound. Tell me what happened."

"OK, I've never told this to anyone before but here goes. Do you know what my name is?"

Carla looked at him with a puzzled look. "I thought I did. I know you as Al Chippingham. What's that, a fake name, and you're really under the witness protection program?"

"No, what I mean is do you know what Al is short for?"

"Not really," Carla said. "I just assumed it was for Albert or Allen, or maybe Alexander. I never really thought about it. Now I'm curious. What is it?"

"It's Alvin. Now think about it. If you put Alvin together with my last name, what is the image that comes to mind?"

Carla scrunched up her face in concentration, and then tried to hide a smile that came out as a giggle.

"Go ahead," Al said. "Say it out loud."

"Alvin and the Chipmunks. I saw the movie with my niece on her eighth birthday in 2007."

"That movie was based on a song from the '50s," Al said. "I grew up hating that song. All of my boyhood friends took delight in making the connection. You can't believe what that did to my self-confidence."

"I'm sorry I laughed," Carla said, "but what does that have to do with God's call?"

"Strange as it sounds, it had a lot to do with it. I was reared by my mother and very insecure about my identity. I was an introvert and felt like I was the butt of lots of jokes. My one defense was that I was pretty smart. I delighted in having the answers before anyone else."

"Thus your ability to argue with the professors and even use Greek and Hebrew terms."

"You got it, but there was always something missing. No matter how many arguments I won, I always knew there was something lacking. Behind my words, I was still that little nerd that everyone laughed at."

"That's why you know what it feels like to be an alien, an immigrant in a foreign land," Carla said.

"I guess that has something to do with it, but I was also rescued from some of that insecurity by an experience I had in a Sunday school class."

"I haven't been to a Sunday school class in twenty-five years at least," Carla said.

Al nodded. "I don't remember much from the Sunday school classes I attended, but I sure remember this one."

"God spoke to you in a Sunday school class?"

"In a way, I suppose that is what happened," Al said, "but I wasn't aware of it at the time. I just knew that I hated my name, and I was a cowardly weakling that everyone laughed at."

Carla made a box with her hands and looked through it at Al. "I'm having trouble picturing that about you, but go ahead."

"I'll need to confiscate that camera later," Al said.

Carla put her hands behind her back. "Not until you finish your story."

"Fair enough," Al said. "The teacher was telling the story of Jacob. I don't know how much you remember about Jacob, but he was a momma's boy, very smart but not very moral."

Carla spoke up. "He's the one that stole his brother's birthright. I remember some things from that Old Testament class."

"More than that," Al said. "He cheated his father, his brother, his father-in-law, and probably anyone else that got in his path. Then one night, according to the Bible, he wrestled with God."

"I often wrestle with God," Carla said, "but I've yet to win many matches."

"Jacob didn't exactly win, either, but he held on to God and wouldn't let God go until God blessed him."

"I like a story where the hare turns on the hound," Carla said.

"I hadn't thought of that," Al said. "What hit me at the time was that Jacob went away from that match with a new name, Israel—and a limp because you don't fight with God without some consequences."

"And that story spoke to you at a really deep level," Carla said in a soft whisper.

"I realized that I could have a new name. I could be Al rather than Alvin and have a new identity as one called by God. It was like a gift of dignity. So I moved from there to thinking about being a pastor."

"I'd say that was pretty dramatic," Carla said.

"It was life-transforming for me but not like what you do. I ended up a pastor of a nice middle-class church and am constantly making compromises just to survive."

"Okay," said Carla. "Quick response, don't even think about it first. Why do you do it?"

"Because grace happens and my people are as desperate for grace as anyone. Although, they don't always . . ." Al stopped in midsentence. He brought his hands together and bent his head in Carla's direction.

"Gee, thanks, Pastor Carla, I think that really is why I do it. Here I thought I was just doing it for the money."

Carla chuckled. "Don't be so hard on yourself. It's not easy being a pastor these days. I may get the media attention for my activities, but I know that you have to fight many quiet battles that no one ever knows about. I also know that you often pay a heavy price for your work."

"Being a pastor is a strange experience," Al said. "I told you what I thought the response would be to your presentation tomorrow."

"I believe your conclusion was that they would sympathize as long as they didn't have to do anything about it."

"We live in an extremely anxious time, Carla." Al paused, reached down into the briefcase at his feet, and pulled out a Bible. He flipped it open and read, "And God said, 'Let there be a dome in the midst of the waters, and let it separate the waters from the waters.' So God made the dome and separated the waters that were under the dome from the waters that were above the dome.'" Al added, "I don't think humanity has ever forgiven God for that act."

"I'm lost," said Carla. "Where in the world are you going with that?"

"Whether it's the Red Sea before the escaping slaves or the stormy sea on Lake Galilee, what do those churning waters always symbolize in the Bible?"

"Ah," said Carla, "that I do remember from seminary. The Hebrews were a people of the land. For them, waters, especially churning waters, symbolized chaos. I remember Dr. Simington pointing out that the opening description of creation was of pure chaos before God spoke and began to draw order out of it."

"That's right," said Al, "and no one likes to live in chaos. We resent it when something stirs up our lives and threatens to burst our thinly veiled bubble of order and security."

"So what does that have to do with the dome?" Then Carla struck her forehead. "Oh, wait, I get it. Even though God built a protection from our being overwhelmed by chaos, God still left a measure of chaos in our lives. God separated the waters above the dome from the waters under the dome. I never saw that before."

"People continue to be frightened by change in their lives. When you ask them to challenge the order of society and question the justice of our system, you are asking them to risk chaos," said Al. "I've always remembered one of our ethics professors saying that when we are frightened enough, we will choose order over justice."

"That explains why so many people tolerate living under dictators," Carla said. "We see our society falling apart, and the dictator promises us order. People like me ask them to risk more chaos."

"Even in a democracy, that's where the resistance comes from," said Al. "Members of congregations like mine want to believe that law preserves order in society, and if we stay out of trouble, all will be well."

"A lot of Latinos don't have the luxury of that bubble of order," Carla said.

"I'm not trying to defend us as pastors," Al said, "but I do think I understand what we are up against."

"But what about the Bible?" Carla pressed. "I remember Jesus castigating the scribes and Pharisees as hypocrites: 'For you tithe mint, dill, and cumin, and have neglected the weightier matters of the law; justice and mercy and faith.' Shouldn't our churches preach that?"

"Yes, but that's the bind," Al said. "Many people in our congregations want to be merciful but only if it doesn't change things too much. They want to cling to the order in society that benefits them— hide under their self-constructed dome, as it were. These are the people who pay the pastor's salary, and, maybe even more important, these are the people who are the pastor's friends."

Carla looked at him for a long time before speaking. "You're caught in that bind too, aren't you? Now I've added to it because of our friendship."

"I'll admit that our friendship adds to the pressure, but there is something deeper than that. Maybe it is not true for you, but I don't know many pastors who don't, at some level, feel they compromise their souls in the very act of being in the ministry."

"I'm not sure I understand," said Carla. "What do you mean they compromise their souls?"

"Look at it this way," said Al. "Congregations can be like hypersensitive lovers. Earlier you spoke of that boyfriend that rejected you. I'm sure you've had plenty of other boyfriends."

Carla looked away as if embarrassed. "There have been a few, but none of them worked out in the end."

"I'm not trying to pry, Carla, but did you ever have a relationship that started out well and then his always wanting more and more began to dominate and drain you?"

"That sounds familiar," Carla said. "I reach a point in which I just have to leave to breathe."

"Sometimes that is the way it is with a congregation. A pastor falls in love with a people," said Al. "At first the pastor thinks the relationship is made in heaven and wants to do things to please them. Then their constant demands begin to chip away at the pastor's passion. He or she feels more used than loved."

"Why don't they leave?" asked Carla.

"Many have," said Al. "They begin with the thrill of being in God's service. They leave because all of the little compromises rob them of the sense of fulfillment in what they do. However, I think even worse are those who learn how to survive by going through the motions in a way that doesn't challenge the security of their congregation."

"And I thought my work had its depressing moments," said Carla. "Don't you reach times when it's just too much?"

"I've thought about that," said Al. "Sometimes it's like Rhet Butler in *Gone With the Wind*. Despite your initial love, you reach a point where you want to say, 'Frankly, my dear, I don't give a diminished F#.'"

"Que barbardidad," she said and playfully punched him in the shoulder. "But you keep hanging in there. Why?"

"For the same reason you keep beating your head against the wall of the immigration problem."

Al saw Carla wrinkle her brow and hesitate.

"I'm not sure I understand," she said.

"We keep wrestling with our faith and demanding that God make sense out of it all. At some level, we recognize that our people also are crying out, trying to make sense out of life."

Carla looked down at the table. "I guess I hadn't seen it from that perspective. It almost makes me feel guilty to stand up and challenge those pastors at our meeting tomorrow."

"Oh, no, don't feel that way, Carla. What you will be saying is important. Even if it is only for a moment, you may pull back the curtain enough for us to glimpse another part of the chaotic world in which God is at work."

"I want justice for my people, but I don't want to get other clergy in trouble." She paused and spontaneously reached out and laid a hand on Al's arm. "I don't want you to lose your job. People need you."

Al reached over and squeezed her hand. "Don't worry," he said. "Most of us are survivors. Besides," he smiled, "that is the real power of the Gospel."

"What do you mean?" Carla asked.

"The compromises that we make are painful. To use Paul's phrase, they are indeed thorns in our flesh. But as Paul also learned, 'God's power is made perfect in our weakness.'"

"See, there you go again, being that brainy guy that I can't always understand."

"No one likes to hear where his life has come up short," Al said. "People want to hear a message that affirms them. Clergy, who are paid by the congregation, feel the pressure to water down the demands of the Gospel. Yet the real gospel keeps tugging at our conscience. We keep hearing that the good news that cost Jesus his life is worth sacrificing for. We dare not lose sight of either. You will help remind us of the gospel message of good news for those who sit in darkness."

"It sounds like a difficult balancing act to me."

"And your life fighting for just immigration procedures and saving people from desperation is such a life of comfort?"

"But that is what God has called me to do," said Carla.

"And God has called me to stand with these people. They aren't evil people. They are just afraid of what it would cost to stand for real justice and mercy. They know life isn't always fair, but they need someone to stand with them and hold their hand as they glimpse the chaos and learn to trust God."

"OK, so help me decide how to make my presentation to presbytery. What can I do to challenge them while also respecting the complex nature of our calls?"

"Let's take a walk. Maybe the fresh air will clear our minds and generate some creative ideas," said Al. He started to reach for the bill, but Carla's hand shot out faster than his and grabbed it.

"I asked for this meeting, so I pay the bill." She rose and started towards the cash register.

"OK, but then I pay for dinner tonight."

She stopped, looked back over her shoulder, and in her best imitation of a Southern drawl, albeit with a Hispanic accent, she said, "Why, Rhett, I do believe you are asking me out on a date. I think that is a C major idea." Then, with a noticeable swing in her hips, she continued towards the cash register.

As they walked out of the coffee house, Al suggested that they head towards a nearby park. The street was filled with blaring horns, an occasional squeal of brakes, and a truck's exhaust that reached to the sky with a grey-blue smoke. Their eyes and ears were buffeted by the busy world.

The sidewalks were crowded, and Al and Carla were silent as each observed the colorful mixture that populated the world around them. A mother with two young children approached on their side of the street. In an attempt to elude the grasp of his sister, one of the children darted in front of them. The mother looked anxious and spoke rapid Spanish to her children, cautioning them to keep close and not to cause other people problems. Accustomed to strangers not speaking their language, the boy retorted that other people shouldn't cause him problems either.

Carla smiled and said, "Hay problemas de mi, niño?

The boy was startled at first and then grinned. "No, Senorita, tu eres tan belleza para hacer problema para me."

"Gracias, hijito, pero debe obedezcer tu mama."

Al chuckled as they walked. They passed a man who wore a turban and a distinctive mark on his forehead. He presented a noble bearing as he entered a limousine. An Oriental couple walked by chattering in a tongue that neither Al nor Carla recognized. Four Caucasian teenagers loudly debated who had the nerve to ask a certain girl to the prom. A homeless man approached and asked them for money. As Al took a bill from his wallet, he asked the man his name and where he was from. They chatted briefly, and then all of them continued their journey.

"That was nice," said Carla. "You treated him like a human being."

"To be honest, sometimes I rush right by, but occasionally I wonder how I would behave if I were homeless and hungry. I think it would make me angry to be treated as if I were invisible."

"It gets tricky," said Carla. "That Hispanic mother back there may want to be invisible because she is afraid she'll be deported. Our homeless friend wants to be visible so that you will have pity and give him some money."

"In different ways," said Al, "they each live in a harsh world. What they want, what we all want, is for the world to hear our cry as a full human being. Even when we are hiding, it is a terrible thing to be invisible."

Carla poked him in the ribs and said, "OK, Bible genius, where was the first cry in the Bible, and who heard it?"

"God heard the cry of the slaves in Egypt and sent Moses to lead them to freedom," Al responded.

"Bong!" Carla made a sound like a quiz show. "Wrong answer, oh learned one."

Al looked puzzled. "Then who was it?"

"It was Abel. Cain had killed him and tried to make him invisible

19

by burying him in the ground. His blood cried out from the ground, and God heard it." Carla did a little skip and punched her fist in the air.

"Hey, that's a great connection," Al said. "Even when the weak are treated as invisible, God still sees them and hears their cry—even as happened," Al continued with a smile on his face, "for those human slaves in Egypt."

"Oh, so we want an instant replay on the official ruling in the contest, do we? If we are going to get nitpicky, I think a case could be made that God heard Sarai's cry when Abram was willing to pimp her out to the Pharaoh."

Al stopped, held up his hands in surrender. "I yield, I yield. You are the winner."

Carla did a little twirl in the street announcing to anyone within range, "Did you hear that. The master of all biblical languages has acknowledged me the winner. Go spread the good news to the world." She continued to giggle with delight as they walked.

Al, pleased, if a little embarrassed at her playfulness, said, "No wonder those border guards are scared of you. When you win you don't take any prisoners."

"It feels good to laugh a little, but we really are facing a difficult task," Carla said. "Actually, it really does fit together. What I want to accomplish is to make sure that the immigrants who are struggling for their lives are not invisible."

"Maybe a way to do that," said Al, "is to help us remember that as clergy we are called by God. What if we were all invited to revisit our call and who it was that called us?"

"As we just did at the coffee house?"

"Yes, even as you talk about the immigration issue, we need to sense the God who called each of us as being present as we respond."

"You mean I can't just guilt them into doing what I want? You're going to take all the fun out of it. Now you want me to know their names, feel their pain, and treat them as human beings too." Carla shook her head in mock exasperation.

They entered the park and left the sounds of the urban street behind. It was spring. Daffodils, narcissus, and cherry trees in bloom sang of life. Carla stopped and gazed at the cornucopia of colors before her. "It makes me sad even as it fills me with delight," Carla said. "This is God's gift to humans. That mother whose death keeps haunting me was denied the freedom to taste creation's wonders. That's just not right."

"Carla, back there in the coffee house, when I was relating to you the events that led to my awareness of God calling me, it was like the distance between God and me was closed, and I was again experiencing God's choice of me as a human being."

"I know," Carla said. "I hadn't relived that experience in the chapel for years, but just for a moment, I remembered again that when all else fails, God has my back."

"Most of the clergy at our meeting would be able to tell you of some moment in time when they felt God's call in their lives," said Al. "Our experience back in the coffee house reminded me how easy it is to lose touch with the power of that sense of call."

Carla stooped to smell some flowers near the path. "I can think better in metaphors," she said. "When you look at these daffodils, what happens for you?"

Al bent beside her and touched the petals gently. "I know it's selfish, but my first impulse is to pick some of them and take them home with me to stay in the presence of their beauty."

"And what happens if you do that?" asked Carla.

"Yeah, I know. If I pick them, I get to use them for my benefit, but they also die quicker."

"I've always believed that God didn't create plants just to be used by humans for food. Rather, God created some plants to expand our souls and fill us with a sense of awe and glory."

"So how does that relate to . . . oh, I get it," said Al. "Like the flowers, many people like to use immigrants and their work to better their lives, but then they toss them aside like wilted flowers."

"Even cut flowers are placed in a vase with water and nutrients," said Carla.

"That's beautiful, Carla, but how do we convey that image to pastors whose congregations are more aware of the laws that are broken by immigrants than by any beauty they bring to the world?"

"This park is protected by laws," said Carla, "and it is important to acknowledge the way that our borders and the laws that define them are necessary, but we also need to remember that real humans, children of the same God who touched us, are involved."

"To be called by God to love a person we fear is quite a balancing act."

"And I need to remember," said Carla, "that some of those neighbors I'm called to love are the clergy that will resist my message."

Over supper with much laughter and storytelling, they developed a strategy for the next day's presbytery meeting.

The next morning they joined with the other clergy as they registered, sipped coffee, and waited for the beginning of the meeting. When they convened and Carla's place on the agenda arrived, Al rose to introduce her.

"Carla Espinoza was in seminary with me. We lost touch over the years. I had the delight of reconnecting with her yesterday. The highlight of our conversation was in recalling our experiences of God's call to ministry and how our different calls were unique but also similar. Carla has come to ask you for support in her ministry among immigrants, but I've asked her to first share her experience of being called by God to her ministry."

As Carla related her story of being drawn to ministry, she spoke of the compelling power of the Gospel that had infused her meek chaplain with a powerful voice so many years ago on the campus of her college.

Then she told the story of arriving too late to save the mother and one of her children. People listened with growing intensity.

A minister from one of the larger churches rose to be recognized. "Your story of the dying mother is very touching, Ms. Espinoza, but, the fact of the matter is, she shouldn't have been there. She was breaking the law. We have laws for good reason."

"I will be glad to respond to that," said Carla, "but Al has taught me that I need to listen more, so first I would like to hear what others of you have to say."

Many of the elders and clergy at the meeting rose to debate the issue before them. It was clear that there was a myriad of opinions and many truly wrestled with the tension between the compassion of their faith and the reality of their lives.

After about thirty minutes of debate, the moderator recognized Carla to speak again. "I want you to know how much I respect the work that you are doing in your churches. It is not easy being a pastor or an elder in these chaotic times. Last night Al asked me why I continued to fight these battles. The issue of law versus mercy is an old one and not to be resolved in today's meeting…"

"But that is the crux of the issue, is it not?" interrupted one pastor.

"It is key," said Carla, "and I don't mean to make light of it. Still, in the eyes of our faith, we've all broken God's law and live under the umbrella of grace and forgiveness."

"But you can't just ignore the law every time someone gets themselves in trouble," said a pastor.

"Let me tell you a story that touches on the very foundation of my faith. Several years ago there was a very cruel border guard who took delight in causing pain for those he caught crossing the border. He went far beyond what even the harshest interpretation of the law permits. In both my eyes and the eyes of the law, he was a lawbreaker."

Carla described some of the actions the border guard had taken and how he had ridiculed her when she protested. "Once, when no one was looking, he even groped me and made lewd suggestions as to what he would do if he ever caught me alone in the desert," she said.

"One day when I was searching for lost victims of the desert's harshness, I came upon him. He, also, had been out in the wastelands searching for lost humans. Only he had a little too much to drink, and he flipped his jeep and was pinned under it. I found him by accident after he had been there for several hours.

"What was I to do? He had caused so many to suffer without remorse, and now he was in my power. All I had to do was drive on. Except that a foundational principle of my faith was that 'while

I was yet a sinner, God loved me.' With no small measure of fear, I called for help and provided him water, stopped his bleeding, and offered care until someone arrived.

"It doesn't always work out this way," said Carla, "but like Paul, that violent enemy of the church, God touched that man, and he has become one of my biggest supporters. You can't anticipate what God will do with even small acts of faithfulness."

There was a silence that filled the room as each person seemed to be examining their own lives and questioning how they would respond in similar circumstances.

The moderator of the meeting spoke up. "Could you summarize what you want from us at this time?"

"Sure," said Carla, "I'm not here to make you feel guilty. I simply want to offer myself as a vehicle by which your churches can reach out to some suffering people. I don't have an answer to the larger immigration problem, but, in the meantime, I want to minister to some of those who have been left by the side of the road. I would be honored if you could support me in that work."

Al spoke again. "What both Carla and I learned last night is that when we struggle with how to respond to the cries of our brothers and sisters, we grow closer to the God who has called us.

"The struggle that each of us face is genuine. God, through Jesus Christ, is always headed towards Jerusalem and the cross. Very good people, like Peter, the head of the church, want to caution us not to place ourselves at risk," Al continued. "But when we, like Peter, despite our denials, still strive to be faithful to the Christ who has called us, we discover again and again that God has our back."

An older man stood to be recognized. He was bent over and had to be helped to his feet. "I've been to these meetings going on forty years, and this was one of the best. We actually wrestled with the Gospel. I'd like to move that this body provide $1,000 to support Ms. Espinoza and also that each of us individually augment that amount with our own personal pledge. I will start with my pledge of $500 and my hope that Ms. Espinoza will return to speak with us about her ministry frequently."

The motion passed unanimously, and $4,000 was gathered in pledges.

When the meeting was over, many people wanted to speak to Carla and assure her of their prayers. Some even asked for more information that they might take back to their congregations.

Al and Carla had parked at the end of the parking lot. Many waved a greeting as they walked to their cars.

"It's going to take me awhile to process all of that," said Al. "I hoped we would get a positive response, but I never expected it to go as well as it did."

Carla looked up to the sky and said, "Well, God, since you are not physically present to receive my thanks, I will have to express it to your messenger."

Al started to ask her what she was talking about when she whirled about, threw her arms around him, and kissed him. When they parted, Carla glanced up to the sky again as if continuing her conversation with God. "I want you to know, God, that that was purely a spiritual expression of my thanks. Although," she hesitated a moment, "I could be convinced to do it again as an expression of love of neighbor."

"Love of neighbor is good," said Al. Then he looked up and saw a few of his colleagues looking their way. "However, perhaps we could revisit this opportunity somewhere away from the church parking lot."

"I'm headed for the airport to catch a plane," said Carla. "It's now or never, Lancelot. Act now, in front of your colleagues, or all may be lost."

Al grinned, shook his head, and then kissed her. "You can catch your plane," he said, "but this is definitely not over."

# 2

## NEVER OFF THE CLOCK

*(Noah was the first to plant a vineyard.)*

It is the end of another long exhausting day. My family is away on a trip, and the house is empty. As I reflect on the day, I have experienced a roller coaster of emotions. When I entered my office this morning, there was an envelope lying on my desk. It was an angry note from a parishioner castigating me for my sermon this past Sunday.

"How dare you assume you have the right to tell me that this nation has the wrong military policy on Iraq," it said. "What makes you think you are so smart? Why don't you stick to the spiritual things you were hired to preach about?"

Criticism always sent me into a tailspin, and I began to berate myself for the poor way in which I had expressed myself when the phone rang. "Pastor," the voice said, "I am at my wits end in dealing with my son, Timmy." I spent the next forty-five minutes counseling a parishioner in need. It felt good to be able to be there and help her process what she was feeling.

After I hung up, I spent the next hour trying to figure out how to interpret the budget to the finance committee. The normal spring and summer reduction in contributions had begun to occur, and I didn't want them to panic. Next, I turned to formatting the bulletin for Sunday, which also meant that I had to come up with a title for the yet unwritten sermon.

I left the office in time to meet a couple for lunch who had expressed interest in joining the church. It was a pleasant lunch filled with affirmations for the ministry they saw taking place at the church. It was especially pleasing to hear the husband say that one of the reasons they were joining the church was that my sermons repeatedly challenged them to relate their faith to the difficult issues in the world around them.

I intended to work on the sermon for the next week when I returned to the office, but my administrative assistant had received word of two parishioners who had been admitted to two different hospitals in the city. I decided that took precedence and left for the hospitals. As I was returning to the church, a transient stopped me with a story about needing money for a bus ticket to get to his brother's funeral. I had learned from experience that the only way to make sure that the money would be used for a bus ticket was to take him to the bus depot and buy the ticket for him. That took the rest of the afternoon.

After a quick supper, I attended the worship committee meeting. What I remember most about that meeting was that we seemed to spend an inordinate amount of time discussing whether we should sing more of the "good old hymns" that would please certain vocal members of the congregation.

Now I am home. The day is over, and I am alone with my thoughts. I remember that my brother had given me a bottle of scotch for Christmas. I decide I need a good strong drink to relax, and I pour myself a double scotch. I miss my family and am feeling slightly sorry for myself. The scotch tastes good. I want to hold on to that feeling a little longer. It is, after all, the end of the day. A second drink seems in order, I tell myself.

Someone once said, "Two drinks are not enough, and three drinks are too many." I'm really feeling the buzz now. To be honest, I'm drunk. I don't really care. I'll just sleep it off. Maybe I'll have a little hangover in the morning, but it really feels good not to pay attention to the boundaries of appropriate behaviors for once.

It's almost midnight when the phone rings. Who could be calling at this hour, I think, as I stumble slightly getting to the phone. I compose myself and make sure that I don't slur my words as I answer.

"This is Pastor Smith. Can I help you?"

"Pastor," the voice was breaking up with intermittent sobs. "This is Dan Foyer. We've been in a terrible car accident. My wife is very serious. We are at the emergency room of Maywood Hospital. Can you please come? We need your prayers."

# 3

## THE GIFT NOT RECEIVED

*(For Cain and his offering God had no regard.)*

"Thank you for calling. I appreciate your honesty. May God bless you. Good-bye." Allen Felkner, pastor of Garden Presbyterian Church, carefully placed the phone in its cradle.

As the phone disconnected, a spontaneous shout erupted from his throat. "DAMN IT ALL TO HELL," he screamed. His fist rose and slammed down on the desk three times as he shouted, "Fuck. Fuck. Fuck."

He was grateful to be the only one in the building at the time. His own language shocked him. It was like the doors of politeness and respectability could no longer contain his anger.

It all started three days earlier. As many good pastors in small churches do, he had developed a system to alert him when normally active members began to lag in their attendance. In a society of loneliness, he had learned, people need to know that they are missed. When he became aware that the Dickersons had not been present the past four Sundays, he called and asked if he could visit them.

He recalled the small sense of foreboding as he rang the doorbell. Mrs. Dickerson smiled a little nervously as she greeted him. "Thank you for coming, Allen. We had meant to call you earlier for a little talk. We appreciate your taking the initiative."

*A little talk*, Allen thought. *This is going to be trouble.* He smiled and extended his hand warmly. "Well, I've been missing you. I wanted to come by and see if there was a problem."

As they chatted, she led him into the living room where Roger Dickerson rose to greet him. Ellen offered them some iced tea as they made uncomfortable small talk. When they were all settled, Roger cleared his throat and began to speak. "Allen, I want you to know that what we are about to tell you has absolutely nothing to do with you. In fact, what makes this so hard is that Ellen and I have so much respect and admiration for you."

Allen's stomach tightened. "If there is something wrong, I certainly want to hear about it. I really care about your whole family and have appreciated your participation at Garden Church."

"It's not that there is something wrong," Ellen said sweetly. "It's just that, well, some friends of ours invited us to go with them to Living Waters Community Church, and we uh" she hesitated, "and we just found their program so inviting for our whole family."

Allen had been in seminary with Harry Harp, the pastor of Living Waters. As a student, Harp was very engaging, always quick with the humorous story. Although Allen was taller, Harp's deep, commanding voice always made Allen feel inadequate. In Allen's mind, Harp was very skilled at self-promotion. Not long after finishing seminary, Harp announced that he was leaving the Presbyterian denomination because it was too confining. With a couple of wealthy families providing the initial backing, he formed the Living Waters Community Church. It grew rapidly into a major church within the community.

The Dickersons described the "fun service" in which the pastor was just an amazing and rather hilarious speaker. They described how their children were almost dancing in the aisles to the lively music of the band and absolutely fascinated by the images projected on the screens throughout the auditorium. Allen couldn't remember the rest of the conversation. He was concentrating on containing his anger as they described the virtues of the Living Waters Community Church.

He said, "This is a big decision. I hope that you will at least pray about it for two or three days and then give me a call." Now he had received that phone call. They had not changed their minds. From a pastoral level, Allen was concerned that a good family was being seduced by a superficial version of Christianity that he believed would not serve them well in the end. It was also a major blow to the Garden church, not only because of their generous financial gifts but also because they had been strong participants in the life of the church.

The Dickersons were just one of several families who had switched from Garden church to Living Waters over the past several years. He released his frustration again, but this time it was not with a curse but with a prayer. "Why, God? Why are you letting this happen? I've tried to be a faithful pastor, and then you let that little weasel, Henry Harp, have all the success."

He recalled a passage from Genesis where Cain and his brother Abel were both making an offering to the Lord, and God accepted Abel's offering but not Cain's. *I think I know what Cain felt like*, Allen thought. If I had my hands around Henry Harp's scrawny little neck right now . . . .

The letter came three weeks later. Allen's hand began to shake as he read it. It was the stone by which he could slay Abel. A disgruntled employee of the Living Waters Community Church had hacked into Henry Harp's computer and printed out a series of torrid emails that Henry had exchanged with a prominent member of his church. It was clear from the emails that Henry was involved in an adulterous affair. He was quite explicit about some of the things that he was doing with his lover and how much he was enjoying plunging into the abyss of lust.

A brief flicker of conscience about reading someone else's mail was quickly suppressed. Allen was still fuming over the loss of the

Dickersons and how Henry Harp's successes spotlighted what Allen felt were his personal failures. Now he held in his hand the power to kill or at least seriously damage Henry's career. The Cain and Abel story wouldn't leave his mind. He remembered God saying to Cain in response to his anger, "Sin is lurking at the door; its desire is for you, but you must master it."

The truth was, at that moment, Allen didn't want to master sin. He wanted to play in the field of this particular sin, savor it, relish it, and taste its full lustful potential. In one corner of his mind, he clearly understood the overpowering seduction of sexual addiction. He knew that he shouldn't give in to this temptation, but he felt almost powerless to resist. On a better day, Allen would have appreciated this experience as an opportunity to deepen his ability to empathize with those who feel trapped in the hold of addiction. But this was not one of those better days. He didn't want to be empathetic. He wanted to exorcise his pain by unmasking Henry Harp for the duplicitous, self-serving hypocrite that he was. The only question was how to do it in a way that would cause maximum exposure.

Allen was so consumed that it took him a moment to realize that his secretary was calling him over the intercom.

"Allen. Allen. Earth to Allen. Come in; come in from wherever you are."

"Huh, oh, sorry, I was thinking about something and didn't hear you. What do you need?"

"Grace is on the phone," she responded with a chuckle.

Grace was Allen's wife. He had often kidded her that he knew the moment he met her that he was saved by grace. Hearing her name interrupted his almost murderous line of thought. He smiled to himself.

"Hi, Grace, what's up?"

"Our neighbor came by with some news. She's a member of your favorite church. They received word today that your seminary buddy Henry has cancer. It's very serious."

"Darn," he responded. "Before you called, I was trying to figure out how to strangle the little weasel. Now I have to feel sorry for him."

"It's tough, Allen, but I thought you ought to know. Love you." She hung up.

As if built into his DNA, Allen didn't hesitate a moment. He dialed the Living Waters church, identified himself as a seminary classmate, and asked to speak to Henry Harp. The secretary's voice broke a little as she told Allen that she would connect him.

Allen could hear the strain in Henry's voice as he answered. The normal upbeat tone was missing. "This is The Reverend Henry Harp. I pray God's blessings on you. With whom am I speaking?"

"Henry, this is Allen Felkner from Garden Presbyterian. We were classmates at Columbia. I know our lives have gone in separate directions since we graduated, but I just heard the news about your cancer and wanted to call and offer my prayers of support. I thought that perhaps it might be of help to talk to another pastor."

"Allen, it's so good to hear your voice. I just got the news this week, and I have to admit I'm still reeling from it all. Let me close my door so that we can talk in private."

Sensing that Henry did want to talk, Allen continued to respond. "How bad is it Henry? What are the doctors telling you?"

"To be honest, Allen, I'm afraid it's going to take one of those miracles that we preachers are always talking about."

Allen could hear Henry take in a deep breath trying to control his emotions.

"Do you have an extra miracle hanging around your church, Allen?" There was a moment of silence, then a clearing of the throat. "I'm having trouble finding one around here right now."

Allen was touched, if a little bit surprised, by Henry's willingness to be so vulnerable. They had never been close, even in seminary. Even though they were in the same city, they had rarely talked since graduation. Yet, at that moment, the barriers had been removed. They were two pastors reaching out to each other. "Henry, I don't have much control over miracles, but I am available for some honest preacher to preacher talk and to have prayers together if that would help."

There was a slight catch in Henry's voice as he spoke. "It

would help, Allen. I know that we have gone down different paths theologically, but right now that doesn't seem to mean very much to me. I remember in seminary that you always seemed to be in touch with something much deeper than I could ever get hold of."

Allen felt slightly embarrassed at hearing Henry's affirmation but recognized that this was Henry's moment to which he needed to respond. "Henry, would you like to meet some place so that we could talk and pray together?"

"Oh, God, would you do that for me, Allen? Could we, uh, could we meet in your sanctuary, just the two of us, and could I, uh, tell you how scared I am? And, and, uh, Allen, would you pray for me right there in that sanctuary? Could you do that for me, Allen?" And then Henry was weeping.

Allen was almost speechless. He knew the whole theory of megachurch growth was to remove all the symbols from what he would call the sanctuary and they called the gathering area. Sermons made brief reference to Scripture but mainly focused on uplifting lessons about life. Music was geared to be upbeat and shaped by the latest trends in the culture. The programs of the church combined entertainment and building supportive life skills together with some opportunities to engage in missions that made the participants feel good about what they were doing. The idea of a prophetic challenge to the materialistic way people were living was considered too negative. But, at this moment, Henry was setting all that aside and crying out for comfort from another pastor in a sanctuary filled with rich symbols of the faith.

"Of course I will do that for you, Henry. When would you like to come?"

There was a slight hesitation. "Allen, I know this sounds ridiculous and exposes me for the hypocrite that I really am, but could we do it late at night when no one else is around?"

Allen wanted to laugh out loud, but Henry's total vulnerability would not allow any but the most compassionate of responses. "Of course, Henry. Look, I don't have a meeting at the church tonight. How about if we meet here about 10 p.m.?"

"Blessings on you, my friend. You are truly a gift from God. I will never forget this." There was a pause, a couple of false starts, and then Henry said, "Uh, Allen, I'm embarrassed to say this, but I don't even know where your church is located."

Allen smiled to himself as he provided Henry with clear directions to the church.

For the next six months, Allen continued to meet with Henry in an almost secretive fashion. Henry talked and Allen listened. Then they would kneel, Allen would lay his hands upon Henry and pray for his healing. After about three months, Henry showed up wearing a long white robe and sandals. "I'm preaching in it," Henry related. "It makes me feel closer to God. I tell people that if it was good enough for Moses and Jesus, then it's good enough for Jesus' servant. Do you think if I get close enough to God, He will heal me, Allen?"

"Henry," Allen responded, "you don't have to wear a robe to curry God's favor. It's your heart that God cares about."

"That's OK for you, Allen, because you're already close to God. I need a sign, something that can prove to me that God is listening. He gave a sign to Gideon, didn't he? Remember how Gideon laid out a sheepskin, and God's making it wet while the ground around it was all dry? Maybe I could put a sheepskin in the worship center. People would really be moved if God made it wet right there in the worship center.

As Allen listened, he realized how dependent Henry was on a success-oriented gospel. He didn't have the resources to sustain him when things went wrong. It made Allen really feel sad for him. For another three months, they continued to meet. Allen listened as Henry mixed messages of fear with dreams of getting a sign from God that would prove to his people that he was God's special friend. Henry would kneel, and Allen would lay his hands on him and pray fervently for Henry's healing.

Then Henry called him in the middle of the day and exuberantly announced that he had his sheepskin. He had just come from his doctor. The doctor told him that his cancer appeared to be in remission. "Allen, I can't tell you how much I appreciate your support during this dark period in my life. I know that you are very busy, and I don't want to take up any more of your time with our meetings. You have truly been God's angel in my time of need, Allen. I will never forget what you have done."

Allen was grateful for Henry's apparent recovery and offered his own prayer of thanksgiving after he had hung up the phone. Somehow he didn't feel as threatened by Henry's successes as he once had. *Though,* he thought, *I wouldn't mind an infusion of fifty new members into the Garden Church as my own sheepskin.*

————————●●————————

Several weeks later, Allen was sitting in his office on Wednesday afternoon working on his sermon for Sunday. His secretary buzzed him announcing that Grace was on the line.

Allen answered with a light-hearted, "My life is centered in grace. What more could I need?"

"I'm not feeling very graceful right now. Are you sitting down?" she asked with a slight edge to her voice.

"Honey, what's wrong?"

"I'm certainly glad that you had to leave early this morning and didn't have a chance to read the paper."

"The newspaper?"

"Yes. It seems that your prayer buddy has taken out a full-page ad announcing that he has been cured of cancer."

"Wow! That's great news."

"Wait till you see the ad. The title in big bold print reads, 'God Is Not Through With Me Yet.'"

"Somehow that sounds like Henry," Allen said with a laugh.

"The ad goes on to quote the Reverend Harp as follows: 'People have often kidded me about my name and asked if I will one day play the harp in heaven. When I learned of this cancer, I thought

God was calling me home. But God met me halfway there and said to me, 'Henry, I still have work for you to do, so I'm sending you back to play the harp of salvation for my people.'"

Allen laughed, "Henry hasn't lost his touch. Still, if the doctors have told him that his cancer is in remission . . . ."

"Oh, you haven't heard the half of it yet. When he announced that God had personally sent him back, it seems that God also told him to build a chapel for healing."

"A chapel?"

"God's Healing Chapel of Living Waters," she said with mounting sarcasm.

"And he took out a full-page ad to announce that to the world?"

"Not just announce it," said Grace with a touch of bitterness. "You remember you told me Henry started wearing a white robe when he came to you for prayer?"

"Yeah, I thought it was a little odd, but it seemed to be meaningful for him."

"I don't know about meaningful, but Henry has figured out a way to make it profitable."

"How's that?"

The ad says Henry, as a thank offering to God for his healing, will give $5,000 towards building the chapel and that any person who will send him a minimum of $1,000 towards the chapel will receive a piece of the robe in which Henry was healed."

"You've got to be kidding."

"Not only that, but he quotes the verse where the woman was healed by touching the hem of Jesus' garment, leaving the distinct impression that Henry's garment may have the same healing power."

Allen said good-bye to Grace and hung up the phone. He pulled out his Bible and turned to the Genesis story of Cain and Abel and read where God had said to Cain, "Why are you angry, and why has your countenance fallen? If you do well, will you not be accepted? And if you do not do well, sin is lurking at the door; its desire is for you, but you must master it."

Strangely enough Allen didn't feel a rush of anger. From the several conversations that he had when Henry was most vulnerable, he realized how frightened Henry was. He was like a little boy always trying to prove himself to a parent whose love he doubted.

He recalled Henry's request for a miracle. Perhaps we both need one. He opened his file drawer, removed the incriminating file on Henry Harper, and slowly fed it into the shredder.

# 4

## THE TEMPTING FRUIT

*1*984, wasn't that the year of George Orwell's *Utopia*, Beth thought as she swung her beat-up Ford Escort into the parking lot of the Waffle House. *It doesn't seem very utopian to me, but it's only February. Maybe things will change. After all Sally Ride made it into space last year, maybe 1984 will be the year of women's progress.*

Beth was meeting Shirley Baker, her friend and mentor for the past three years. She treasured her friendship with Shirley who had been paving the way for women in ministry over the past fifteen years. They were celebrating Beth's third anniversary as associate pastor of Third United Methodist Church.

As Beth entered the restaurant, a waitress called out, "Welcome to Waffle House." The smell of bacon and the sizzle of eggs as they hit the griddle also greeted her. She joined Shirley in a booth with a faded, laminated tabletop. Shirley greeted her with a big smile. "It's great to see you, Beth. How does it feel to have survived your first three years in ministry?"

"I'll know better when I meet with the Pastor-Parish Relations Committee next week. Every time I meet with them, I feel like I'm meeting with my father. No matter what I do, it is never quite good enough. There are times when I 'm ready to can the whole thing."

Shirley nodded in sympathy. "I know it's not been an easy three years, Beth, but you've done a very good job. The bishop didn't offer you a cushy assignment. He knew there was resistance to a woman as pastor, but I think he was right that you are just the person to help break down their prejudices."

The waitress appeared, and Beth decided to splurge and ordered a waffle and a scrambled egg along with coffee. "Oh, what the heck," Shirley said, "I'll have the same."

When the waitress left, Beth continued, "I suppose I should be grateful for the Methodist placement system where the bishop can put pressure on a church to accept a woman. If I were a Baptist, I might never get a job."

"How's old Amos treating you? He's no prophet, but I assume he's generally a pretty fair boss. He's convinced the bishop to let him stay at that church for ten years now. Probably because he doesn't make waves, and he convinces the parish to make decent contributions to the annual conference each year."

"He's alright. He didn't want a woman associate when the bishop first suggested it three years ago, but I think it was more about not wanting to have trouble in the church than anything he had against women pastors. He knew it was time, though, and as long as the bishop took the heat for suggesting the idea, he went along with it."

"Bottom line, he's a company man and does what's expected of him."

"Other than being a little paternalistic, I really think he's fairly nice. Sarah, his wife, sort of keeps him in line. I sometimes think she would have been the better pastor. Aside from her, though, I 'm not getting a whole lot of support from the women in the church, especially the older ones."

"Not surprised. Most of us have learned to adjust to life as it is. Threaten to change things, and it means that we all have to reevaluate who we are. Familiar pain is more comfortable than the unknown future."

"I can understand that for the older women, but it is even true for some of the women who have been professionally successful.

Take Theresa Ingram, for example. She is vice president of a major insurance company. You know that wasn't easy to achieve. She is always on my back. It's never direct and is often in the guise of trying to be helpful, but there is always the subtle message that I 'm not quite good enough."

"Like the shorts under your robe incident that you told me about?"

"Yeah, what difference does it make whether I wear shorts or a dress under my robe? Who's going to know the difference, anyhow? I just didn't feel like wearing panty hose that day. I've seen Amos wear mismatched socks, and no one calls him up and complains. They just chuckle about his lack of color coordination and go on."

"Now tell me, honestly, Beth, wasn't wearing shorts under your robe that Sunday just a little bit of the rebel coming out in you?"

Beth smiled sheepishly. "Well, maybe a little. But I still think they're just trying to find fault. I work hard at being a good pastor. Why won't they cut me some slack?"

"You mentioned Theresa's lack of support. What's really going on there?"

"I don't know. To be fair, most of her criticisms are well meant. It's just that the compliments don't come as often as the critique. I've told you about how she lost part of her leg in an accident a couple of years ago."

"Yes."

"Well, I think she's being protective of the congregation that supported her during her recovery. Since they didn't really want a woman pastor, she wants to make sure that they don't get hurt by what she refers to as 'the experiment.'"

"'The experiment!' That sounds like you are some kind of test-tube baby or something."

"I think I 'm the 'or something. '"

The conversation continued for another hour. Beth felt better just having someone with whom she could talk.

It was almost ten when Beth finally arrived at Third United Methodist Church. The large brick building, built during the heyday of the '50s, was showing its age. The trustees can't keep delaying repairs because the budget is tight, thought Beth. A shabby-looking church can discourage new members from coming.

She walked down the dimly lit hallway towards the office suite and was warmed by the office lights. Faithful Lucy was working away even though the pastor, Amos, was away on a brief vacation. Lucy Bevil was a delightful, if slightly cynical, Episcopalian that Beth always felt was a breath of fresh air. As she entered, Lucy looked up, "Hi, Beth. Say, since Amos is away, how about you and I stirring up some minor revolution? It's always so much fun to see him scurrying around tamping out the fires."

Beth laughed. "Lucy, I do wonder at times if there wasn't a typo on your job application, and your last name should have begun with a D rather than a B."

"Tell that to the rascal I married. Though I will admit that he can be a devil at times. On second thought, the way things are going in the Episcopal Church these days, if they ever found out that one of their members was Lucy Devil, they would be sure that it was really Lucifer."

"Anything happen around here that I need to know about?"

"With Amos on vacation and your being away for two days, other than the poker game I hosted here, it's been pretty quiet. You do have a message to call Louise Johnson. She's worried that her poor little Bobby is being too stressed by all the work expected in his confirmation class. After all, that's just about exploring what it means to be a Christian. It certainly shouldn't interfere with his soccer and TV time."

"I have an idea, why doesn't Lucifer call her back and tell her that you have a prior claim on her son and you support her desire to water down his Christian training?"

"Now who's got the devil in her?"

"I think I need to get to work on the sermon and prepare a nondemanding confirmation class for next Sunday."

Preparing a sermon was always a challenge for Beth. While she didn't think Amos was a great preacher, she was impressed with his ability to turn them out Sunday after Sunday despite all of the demands of overseeing the functions of the church and managing the competing interests of the congregation. It usually took her at least twenty hours to prepare.

She was still fuming about the email she had received about her last sermon. The writer thought that she was a little shrill, a word that she couldn't imagine being used about a male preacher. As a longtime member, he wanted to remind her that this congregation was made up of good people who needed to be praised for their good works and not told that they had failed to reach out to a lot of likely undeserving vagrants and illegal immigrants. The very idea of suggesting that our dear Lord and Savior might have been an illegal immigrant when his family fled to Egypt was just insulting.

Beth was focused on the research for her sermon when Lucy buzzed her to tell her that she had a phone call. When Beth picked up the phone, a young woman hesitantly asked if she was the pastor of the church.

"I'm the associate pastor. Amos Forrester, the pastor, is away. What can I help you with?"

"Well, I'm Emmy, and my fiancé and I want to get married in June. We were wondering if we could do it at Third United Methodist Church?"

"I gather that you are not a member here," Beth said.

"No, we haven't been going to church since we moved here. We visited when my family was in town over the holidays, and you have such a lovely sanctuary. It looks just perfect for our wedding. I guess we could join, if that were a requirement."

"No, we do conduct weddings for nonmembers. What you would need to do is schedule the date with our administrative assistant, and then we would need to set up a series of three premarital counseling sessions."

Beth noticed that Emmy hesitated, cleared her throat, and then asked, "Uh, is it possible that Reverend Forrester could conduct the service? I mean, well it's just that my fiancé is a little traditional, and he thinks that pastors should be men."

Beth felt angry but tried her best to control her voice as she responded. "Actually, Reverend Forrester is away on vacation this week. You would have to call back later and see what his schedule is."

Emmy seemed relieved. "OK, I'll call back next week. I appreciate your understanding."

"I didn't say that I understood," Beth replied. "And I am not sure that Reverend Forrester will either, but I don't speak for him. For your sake, however, I would make sure that this is just an archaic quirk in your fiancé's personality and doesn't extend to a lack of respect for women in other areas as well."

"Oh, no, he is a wonderful person. I think this just comes from the family in which he was reared."

Beth noticed just enough hesitancy in Emmy's voice to wonder if she had not identified an issue that the couple would have to deal with in the future. She didn't press. She understood that ministry at this point was just to plant the seed and leave it to God to nurture the growth. "I'm sure that he is, Emmy. Why don't you call next week and talk to Reverend Forrester. In the meantime, while it is not a requirement for having your marriage here, I would encourage you and your fiancé to start attending worship. It's a great way to build your relationship."

"I will talk to him about it, and thank you for being so understanding."

As Beth hung up, she yelled through the door to Lucy, "That was a prospective bride who wanted to use, and I do mean use, our church for her wedding because it is so lovely. Her fiancé, even though he doesn't attend any church, considers it improper for women to be pastors. It's at times like these that I wish I were an Episcopalian rather than a Methodist. I think a good strong scotch might calm my nerves."

"Now, now, John Wesley might frown on thoughts like that. Even if he didn't frown, I'm afraid your vaunted Pastoral-Parish Relations Committee would."

———◆•◆———

Beth spent the next hour working on her sermon. Lucy came to the door with a concerned look on her face. "Beth, it's Sarah. She didn't say what, but I think there may be a problem."

Beth picked up the phone. "Sarah, it's Beth. What's going on?"

Pause

"Skiing! When did this happen? How bad is it?"

Pause

"A heart attack! Oh Sarah, I'm so sorry. Where is he? Is he going to be all right? Is he conscious?"

Pause

"How are you doing? Is there someone there with you?"

Pause

"Yes, Sarah, I have a pad of paper right before me. Why don't I put Lucy on the other line so that she can take notes too?" Lucy hurried into her office and picked up the phone. "We're both on now, Sarah. Go ahead."

Beth scribbled the various things that Amos had told Sarah needed to be taken care of. Sarah, being a very acute observer of church life, added a few additional suggestions herself.

When they hung up, Beth sat there for a few moments in a daze. Lucy came back to the door. "I'm not really serious, but I bet that scotch sounds even better now. I didn't hear the first part of the conversation. How is he doing?"

"Apparently, he went skiing with his son, and as they were coming down the slope, Amos lost control and hit a tree. He broke a leg in the process, but, even worse, it seems that the stress of the event caused him to have what they hope is a minor heart attack. He's conscious, and they have taken him by ambulance to a nearby hospital."

Beth grimaced. "OK, here is what we have to do. I have to talk with the district superintendent first. After that, I will need to talk with the lay leader, Ben Fielder. He's a banker at Community Trust. Please get his number for me. After that, I will need to talk with Theresa Ingram as head of the Pastor-Parish Relations Committee. We will have to postpone that meeting and have a special meeting of the church council instead."

"How long do they think he'll be out?"

"They aren't sure at this point, but it could be as much as four to six months."

"You know you can count on me, Beth. If you have a weakness, it's that you try to do everything yourself. Be smart and ask for help. I think you'll be surprised how even some of your critics will rally around at a time like this."

"Thanks, Lucy. I really appreciate your support."

Beth called her district superintendent, Russell Bedford, and shared what had happened. He was very direct with her. "Beth, here are the choices we have. First, there is no guarantee that Amos will be back in six months. Second, let's assume for a moment that he will be. How do we handle the next six months? As I see it, there are a couple of possibilities. One, I could find a retired pastor who would fill in for Amos. Or two, we could put you in charge and find a retired pastor who would serve as your temporary associate."

"Russell, you know that this church only accepted me because the bishop twisted their arms really hard. How do you think they would respond if I suddenly were in charge?"

"That's not the most important question, Beth. The primary question is what would you like? I'm going to hang up now and call you back in about two hours. During that time, I want you to deeply and prayerfully consider what you think both you and God want. I'm not trying to lay a piety trip on you, but I do believe that God can use unusual circumstances to accomplish God's purposes. I'd like to have an emergency meeting of the council on Saturday morning at 10 a.m. Whichever way you answer, we have a lot of work to do." With that, Russell hung up.

As she hung up, Lucy came over the intercom. "I know you have plenty on your plate, but I thought you would like to know that that young Fletcher couple you married shortly after you came here just called from the hospital to announce that they are parents of twins."

"I need to get out of this office and clear my head. I can't think of a better way to do that than celebrate with the Fletchers their double bonus."

———————◆●———————

The couple burst into wide grins when they saw Beth enter their room. "Come see what we have," they cried. Beth had the pleasure of saying the first prayer to welcome two healthy children into the world.

"You get part of the credit," Tommy said.

"Tommy's right," Lila agreed. "Without your support and counseling, I'm not sure we would have gotten this far. The boy will be Thomas, Jr., but we've decided to name the girl Elizabeth after you."

For once Beth was speechless, but the tears flowing down her cheeks were message enough for the Fletchers. As Beth entered the elevator a few minutes later, she noticed a poster on the elevator wall of a set of smiling nurses and words that said, "We can train our nurses with the technical skills, but their capacity to care is a gift from God."

———————◆●———————

The church council convened on Saturday morning. While they were milling around getting their coffee and doughnuts, Beth was surprised at how many came up and assured her of their support.

At about 10:15, Russell convened the meeting. He shared the latest information about Amos and Sarah. Someone immediately asked what the church could do.

Russell handed out a paper with Amos and Sarah's address on it. "I encourage all of you to drop them a note. At least for a couple of weeks, until Amos is strong enough to travel, they are going to feel cut off from the people they love. Handwritten notes can mean a great deal. When they do come home, they will need to monitor how many visitors they have. I would suggest you ask a close friend of Sarah's to coordinate your offers of help."

"How long is he going to be out?"

"It is hard to know for sure, but it will be at least several months."

"So what do we do in the meantime?" another deacon asked.

"I've had several conversations with Beth and with your lay leader, Ben Fielder, and we feel there are a couple of options."

Following Russell's description of the options before them, several people spoke up. Most of the conversation affirmed Beth's ministry but then questioned whether she was ready to assume the responsibility of being the pastor.

Then Theresa Ingram spoke up. "I have chaired the Pastor-Parish Relations Committee and have worked closely with Beth these past three years. As she can tell you, I've been concerned about whether Beth was the right person to be an associate pastor at this church. However, two things have changed my mind. First, in the last couple of days, I have watched Beth take charge in preparing for this meeting. The circumstances, in my opinion, have brought out the best of Beth's leadership qualities. Second, I started thinking about Beth's ministry to me during my recovery from my accident and have watched her minister to others as well. What I want most in a pastor is the ability to convey God's compassionate love at times of need. I think if you will reflect on it, you will agree that Beth has grown in her capacity to do that during her time with us."

Russell then invited Beth to speak to the group.

"I do have something to say, but before I do, I would like to lead you in prayer for Amos and Sarah as well as for this church that we might discern what it is that God wants from us."

After the prayer, Beth scanned each of their faces in silence. Then she began to speak. "It's no secret that when I came here three years ago, there were many that did not want to have a woman as their associate pastor. Yet over those three years, many of you have entrusted me with your pains and joys. I've held your hands at times of tragedy and danced at the weddings of your children."

"You sure out danced most of us at my daughter's wedding," someone said. There was a general ripple of laughter.

"I went to a good seminary," Beth continued, "but I've learned far more from you these past three years than I ever did in seminary."

"We're just a fountain of knowledge," someone quipped.

"Yeah," said another, "knowledge of good and evil."

"Actually," said Beth, "that is the temptation that you face at seminary. You think you have all this knowledge about what is right and wrong for the church. You come to a congregation and discover that only God knows the truth about good and evil. What you have to do is care about the people and trust God.

"When I called Russell and told him about Amos' situation, he asked me to think about what I wanted and what I thought God wanted. So here is what I've decided."

You could sense the quiet intensity with which everyone was now listening.

"While I want to be your pastor, I honestly don't know if I have the skills and the experience to be the pastor of this church," Beth paused.

Theresa again spoke up, "I think Beth may be right. She may not have the knowledge and skills to pastor this church. However, I believe that together we have the skills and experience. I think this might be God's challenge for us at this moment in time."

"What's the history of a woman being pastor of a church this size?" one of them asked.

"I'm not trying to be cute," Russell said, "but you might remember that Jesus chose a woman, Mary Magdalene, to be the first person to experience the resurrection and to spread the word to the rest of the disciples."

"If I remember the biblical story correctly," said one female deacon, "that happened because the male disciples had run away because they were scared."

"The truth is," said Beth, "I'm scared. If you agree to this, I'm going to need your help."

"You were there when my Peter was getting into trouble. I'm not sure we would have handled it right if it weren't for you. You may not handle everything right either, but we will be there for you just like you have been there for us."

There was a general murmur of agreement.

"I'll admit," said Ben Fielder, "that as lay leader I was none too thrilled when Amos came to me and told me that you were coming. Yet I've watched you and Amos work together, and I think you make a pretty good pair. Amos can be a little stodgy at times, and you've brought some new vitality to us, not to mention a few new members who like your style. I'm with you, Beth, all the way. We may have been late to the party, but I'll bet that though some in this congregation may not have wanted a woman to be their pastor, all but the most hardheaded of them will want you to be their pastor."

# 5

## DID GOD SAY?

"Want some grapes, Eve?"

"No, I think I want a big luscious tomato spiced with some red peppers."

"Sure thing, Eve, I might have to stroll a couple of hundred paces to get that. I'll just eat this succulent peach while I walk."

I often wondered what they did all day long–Adam and Eve, that is.

Here they were living a life of abundance. Day after day, all they needed was available. Beyond a little cultivation and deciding among the choices, there was little they had to do. Of course it involved work, but once you fall into a routine, even demanding work fails to stimulate you.

Do you think it might have been boredom that got them into trouble? I think that might have been my problem. Like Adam and Eve, I knew the broad outlines of what God expected of me. I was called by God to be a pastor.

What a thrilling thought to be working for God. However, when your call results in being a pastor of a modest-size church in a small Midwestern city, the work can become rather tedious.

I know the old joke about only having to work one hour a week, but the congregation seems more than willing to fill in the rest of the hours as well. Two or three nights a week, there is some committee meeting. During the day, there are hospital visits to make, Bible studies to conduct, youth groups to plan for, community work with other pastors, and responding to the inevitable family crisis or personal counseling.

At first, your spouse is supportive, but she can easily tire of shouldering most of the responsibility for the home front. I know many other professions are demanding, but at least a doctor's spouse has some extra money to ease the stress of loneliness and to care for the children's needs. Knowing that you are called by God does have a special satisfaction, but it does not pay very well.

Marie and I never fought a lot, but when we did, it was often about money. When the prosperous businessman, who despite his high income did not give as much money to the church as we did, complained that the church budget could not afford a raise in the pastor's salary, it did not contribute to a pleasant atmosphere at home. It did not feel good to come home after a long day of responding to other people's needs and find your daughter in tears and your wife stony-faced because she had just explained that we could not afford to send our daughter to camp with her best friend that summer or to buy her a personal iPhone.

It stung the night Marie lashed out and said, "When God called you to the ministry, did God explain that you were being called to be poor and to deny your family members the comforts of life?" I did not help matters by piously suggesting that there were many people in the world who were far worse off than we were. Her response was sweet but deadly.

"Oh, Charles, I'm so sorry. I did not realize that the purpose of denying you a raise in salary was to raise the economic level of the impoverished of the world. Silly me, I thought it was a choice between you and the congregation's plan to redecorate the parlor for the third time in ten years."

It made me feel like less of a man when I could not provide for my family. Marie would agree that neither of us dreamed of being rich. We just wanted not to have migraines each month as we tried to stretch my small paycheck to meet our many bills. Occasionally we wanted to afford some little extras.

I think that was really how it began. Marie's birthday was coming up. I wanted to surprise her with a nice night out–baby sitter, dinner, and tickets for a play at the community theater. I wanted to make her feel special for one night and know that I did appreciate all she endured with patience.

I looked on it as a loan. I was left to clean up after worship and put the money from the offering in the church safe until the treasurer could count it on Monday morning. A local high school choir sang in our worship service, and there were several parents of the choir members in attendance. That resulted in more cash than normal in the offering plates. To borrow $150 to help my wife feel special did not seem like an evil thing to do.

The problem was it worked like a charm. Marie was thrilled. I felt like her hero, and the church was not hurt at all. In fact, I reasoned, those parents were there because I worked so hard with the church youth group who suggested the idea. In a way, it could be seen as an extra bonus for all I was doing.

The next time it was to buy Christmas gifts for the family. After all, they were the ones who paid the extra price for my long hours. After that, it was an Easter outfit for my daughter and a Wii program for the whole family. It was not long before the loan/bonus program amounted to several thousand dollars.

Marie never asked any questions, my children were happier, and not long after that I received a call to another church. This church had tighter controls on the offering plate, offered a slightly higher salary, and had a discretionary fund that was totally under the pastor's control. It was intended to enable the pastor to respond to the needy that came to the church for help and discreetly to help members who found themselves in crisis. Occasionally, I found that it was my family who had the need.

I must admit there was also a little thrill to the clandestine nature of my efforts. It was very easy to lose awareness that you were working for God and feel ground down by the continual demands of the ordinary events in ministry. Each month you produced at least four bulletins and sermons, planned youth meetings, prepared a newsletter, visited the sick, listened to the woes of the elderly, and moderated several meetings that seemed to accomplish very little. Occasionally there was a crisis or some conflict that got the juices going, but mostly the work was routine.

I have read news articles about politicians, financial wizards, lawyers, and CEOs of large corporations getting caught accepting bribes or engaging in creative and profitable money-making schemes. These were not people who were living in poverty. I often wondered what made them risk everything to get a little bit more when they already had enough.

I think I understand now. It was not about the money. It was the thrill of living on the edge. It was sort of like an addiction. It began with some small rationalization that justified my actions. Then there was the thrill of getting away with it. It made me feel smarter than others. Then, like dope, the old thrill was not enough. You had to raise the stakes, take more risks, and prove to yourself how brilliant you really were.

While you yearned to tell someone else so that they could admire how clever you were, you could not really do that. So you became a god, creating your own little universe and setting your own standards of right and wrong. (You had eaten the fruit of the knowledge of good and evil.) If you gave the appearance of success, others would praise you, but none could fully know who you were.

The kids are now in college. Marie has withdrawn into a little shell. We live with a silent agreement never to discuss the source of the money. I have learned that religion sells, and the Internet expanded the market.

In the beginning, I believed I was being called to be part of God's team to save the world. Somewhere that connection got lost. Maybe it was when I began to create my own little universe. At first, it was for a good cause. I wanted to make Marie and the children happier. It felt good to please them. Soon my ego was stroked not only by their admiration but by my own shrewdness. Also there was the adrenalin of taking a risk. It made me feel alive.

How long will it last? I am not sure that an addict ever asks that question. They only focus on the next high. I am speaking at a religious convention next week in Las Vegas. The title of my speech is "God didn't create this rich earth and then call you to be poor."

I've also been studying how to win at the black jack table. Most people think it all depends on luck, but I think I have discovered a method that just might work.

# 6

## A FAMILY THING

The Duke Clergy Health Initiative documents the dramatic decline in the health of clergy in recent years. It is critical, therefore, for both clergy and congregations, that we identify ways to counter the stresses of ministry. The pressures on clergy do not affect them alone. Stressed out clergy impact their congregations and their families.

As an example of one way that a clergy can measure the discomfort his or her ministry is causing the family, I have included a family game that the whole family can play. It is as fun way to have an important conversation.

Members of a pastor's family, especially the children, rarely have the opportunity to hear how other pastor-families view the experience. If your family enjoys the game, you might explore the idea of playing the same game with another pastor's family. Everyone might be surprised about what they hear from the mix of the families.

An additional benefit is that now they will be acquainted with another family that understands what they are experiencing.

## Family Game

This game is meant to facilitate conversation about the church and the ministry among the family. Make it a fun night with special food, perhaps music, and maybe even a prize for the best answer at the end of the game.

Get a pack of 3 x 5 cards and develop some probing questions to place on each of the cards. Shuffle the cards and put them face down as a deck on the table. When it comes to a person's turn, the player rolls a die and the number on the die determines how far down the deck the player counts to pull the question to be answered. Each time a question is answered, bury the card back in the deck before the game continues.

Some sample questions might be:

1. Describe a time this past year when you were glad that you were part of this family.
2. Talk about a pressure you felt because the minister of the church is part of your family.
3. Share something that happened at the church this past year that made you proud to be part of the church.
4. Describe something that either did or would make you angry when it happened at the church.
5. Identify either a difficult person or situation at the church for whom you think the family should pray.
6. Was there a time this past year when the congregation needed the pastor and it meant that some family experience needed to be changed? How did you feel about this?
7. Whether you are the pastor or a family member, name four things that are good about being a pastor.
8. Whether you are the pastor or a family member, name four things that make being a pastor difficult.

9. If you were to pray for one thing to change in your family, what would it be?
10. What are some fun things that you like to do with the family?

You can, as a family, compose 10--20 more questions and agree that family members can always add more questions to the deck at any time.

# 7

## TRUTH AND CONSEQUENCES

*A Pastor Confronts Sexuality (It is not good that the man should be alone.)*

She appeared in the doorway of my office. She was dressed in a conservative pants suit that made her look professional but did not hide the fact that she was an attractive woman. Her face seemed to alternate between a look of fear and anger, as if it couldn't decide which should triumph.

"My name is Eleanor. We've been attending your church lately. I know that I don't have an appointment, but I need to talk with you."

Clergy are always caught in the bind of wanting to be accessible but at the same time needing periods of uninterrupted time to accomplish a myriad of other tasks. Some use their secretary or an irritating electronic voice offering a variety of button options in order to protect their privacy. Having experienced the frustration of trying to get past such barriers myself, and perhaps not wanting the church's message to be one of unavailability, I chose to keep my office door open to all visitors. Sometimes, when a sermon or preparation for an important meeting was near, I wondered at the wisdom of such a choice.

When I saw the look on her face, I was glad that she didn't have to wind through a labyrinth to find a human ear. There is always a touch of panic that my skills will prove inadequate when someone comes to me in need, so I uttered a silent prayer and rose to greet her. I tried to project a warm and welcoming smile.

"Please come in. You do look like you need to talk with someone."

She was a brunette. I would guess about five-foot-eight inches with dark brown eyes. Though I'm guessing, I placed her at about forty-five years of age, but her face reflected such strain that at another time, she might have appeared younger. She forced a smile of acceptance as she entered my somewhat cluttered office and immediately accepted my offer of a chair in the guest area of my office. I would have offered her some coffee, but she didn't give me time to speak the words.

With no preamble, she began. "Do you remember the sermon that you preached several weeks ago about telling the truth and healing your soul?"

I confess, as I've heard many preachers admit, that once a sermon is preached, I quickly put it out of my mind as I begin to focus on what is next. Besides, I hadn't preached for too many years before I realized that what people hear can be at wide variance with what I thought I had said. When someone wants to comment on a past sermon, particularly one preached several weeks in the past, I often make some vague response in hopes that what they say next will jog my memory, and I won't appear to be a complete dolt.

"Why don't you tell me what you heard in the sermon and why it stayed with you?"

"Oh, it stayed with me, all right. I don't think I will ever forget it. It may well have destroyed my marriage."

I'm sure there was a look of shock on my face as I tried to think of how to respond. I try to apply the Scriptures to the real issues that people face, and I am normally prepared for occasional negative, even angry, responses. This time, however, the response seemed to be more of vulnerable despair than defensive anger. "Tell me what happened," I said.

"You were speaking on the Scripture passage, 'You shall know the truth and the truth will set you free.' You started talking about the burden of secrets; how the energy to protect them drains you; how such hidden thoughts eat away at your soul. I think you mentioned something about shouting the message from the roof tops and the healing experience of no longer having to protect yourself and your secrets."

She paused, as if to gather up her courage, and then continued. "I noticed during the sermon how my husband, Harold, was more restless than usual. He was never one to sit quietly for a long time, but he seemed particularly uneasy that morning. I reached out and put my hand on his leg, and he jumped as if I had touched him with an electric probe. He brushed my hand away but didn't look at me.

"I don't know what you said in the rest of the sermon. I hope it was good. I couldn't listen. I knew that my husband had some huge secret, and my mind raced ahead thinking of all the possibilities. I thought the service would never end. We slipped out the side door." A small smile came to her face. "Our children didn't understand why we weren't waiting in line to shake your hand. They always seem to enjoy that part. I think it's because you always treat them like real people."

She took a breath and let it out slowly. "Anyway, we drove in silence while our children chattered about what had happened in Sunday school and what they wanted to do that afternoon. I'm sure that I didn't sound as casual as I was trying to, but I suggested that as a treat we stop at a MacDonald's and grab a happy-meal for each of them. Then we could let them go to the community pool for the afternoon."

I felt a need to say something, even if it was merely a bridge comment. "I bet they liked that suggestion."

She nodded and thinking about her children brought a small smile to her face. "Yes, that was one time that I was glad that children of that age tend to be self-absorbed. They didn't pick up on the tension that was in the front seat. My husband barely said a word."

Her face colored. "I'm sorry," she suddenly said, "but when I am really nervous, I get a loose bladder. I need to go to the bathroom. I'll be right back."

She left the room as I sat there stunned by her story and wondering what would come next.

While she was gone, I quickly grabbed a notebook and made some hasty notes. I didn't know what was coming. Even though I never take notes while I'm listening to someone tell me their concerns, I find that writing my initial thoughts can help me organize my thoughts.

She returned, smoothed her slacks as she resumed her seat. "Let's see," she said, "where were we?"

I was still slightly off balance but managed to offer, "I think that you had just left your children at the community pool."

A look of pain crossed her face. "Yes, well that was the beginning of the longest afternoon of my life. After we dropped the children off at the pool, my husband said, 'I guess that we need to go somewhere where we can talk.'

"His face was like a stone sculpture, and he would not look at me.

"I decided there was no value in pretending I didn't know what he was talking about, so I said, 'Harold, I don't know what happened at church, but I'm guessing that you have been trying to hide something from me and something in the sermon hit a release valve.'

"'I guess that was pretty close to it,' Harold said. 'It's just as well. It's been driving me crazy for a couple of months.'

"My body was so tight I thought it would crack if I moved a muscle. What happened that could make my previously warm husband freeze up like that? The last couple of months flashed through my mind."

She looked embarrassed but plunged ahead. "I realized that we hadn't had sex for a very long time. That had to be it, I thought, Harold had fallen in love with someone else. I realized that I was holding my breath and felt as if I was about to faint. I gulped for air and finally was able to say, 'Whatever it is, we have to talk about it.'

"'Yeah, I know,' he said. 'Let's go home and talk there.'

"We drove in silence, entered our house, and moved towards the family room. The irony hit me that we were going to a room that we called the family room to talk about an event that might destroy our family."

She looked at me with an accusing eye. "I'm not sure that the truth will set you free," she said.

"It can cause great pain," I agreed.

She lifted her chin as if to force herself to continue. "We sat down in the family room. Harold was all bent over, looking at the floor. 'El,' he began, 'I do love you and the children, and I have never felt so worthless in my whole life. I have seriously considered killing myself but just didn't have the guts.'

"I'm now convinced I know what is coming, and I am angry. 'Who is she?' I asked.

"Then came the bomb shell. He looked up at me and with more pain than I think I have ever seen in a person's eyes. He said, 'That's the problem. It isn't another woman.' Then, in almost a whisper, he said, 'It's a man.'

"What!" I screamed. I went a little crazy and called him a fag and a number of other words that I'd rather not repeat. In your sermon, you said the truth shall set you free. Well, as far as I'm concerned, the truth is that my husband is going straight to hell, and there is nothing I can do about it. Even if it is true, it's a truth that I wished I'd never heard."

I remember feeling very frightened that I might say the wrong thing. I knew for certain that I had to avoid getting defensive about what she had heard in the sermon. This was not about me but about her. "Eleanor," I said, "I can't take back the sermon, but I can help you think this through if you are willing to talk about it some more."

Her face again contorted in a mixture of agony and despair. "Ever since I was a child, the church has told me that I was supposed to believe in the Bible. I know we have just started coming to your church, but I've heard several preachers on TV and in other churches make it pretty clear. If the Bible is right, then my husband is going to hell. I don't know what there is to talk about."

I think sometimes as we engage in the theological debate about homosexuality in the church, we forget that real people and real pain is being felt among our members. I felt a small twinge of anger at some of my more vocal colleagues as I tried to speak. "Let's separate things out a bit. At this moment, are you angriest at me for the sermon, the Bible, or your husband?"

The question seemed to interrupt her spiraling despair. She stared at me for a long time. It was as if trying to sort it out calmed the fury and let her mind focus. Then she smiled ruefully and said, "I'm not letting any of you off the hook, but let's start with the Bible."

I felt a little calmer. Now we were back in my territory. I'd wrestled a lot with what the Scriptures say about homosexuality. I admit it's confusing, but I thought I could help.

"Eleanor, I've studied the passages in the Bible that make reference to homosexuality. There are only about six or seven of them, and they're not as clear-cut as many would have you believe."

"Didn't God destroy Sodom and Gomorrah because they were filled with homosexuals?"

"The Bible makes clear that the people in those cities weren't very nice people. The prophet Ezekiel said that God destroyed them because, although God had blessed them with wealth, they refused to take care of their poor, and they showed abysmal hospitality towards the stranger in their midst."

"They wanted to rape some men, didn't they?"

"Yes, they did. The little book of Jude, in the New Testament, suggests that their real sin was crossing the fixed boundaries God had set. They threatened to have sex with angels."

Eleanor shifted in her chair. It was clear that while the discussion of the Bible had been a distraction, it wasn't what really concerned her.

"Well, you know more about the Bible than I do, but I don't think that Jesus approves of my husband being a queer."

"Jesus never said anything about homosexuality, but he did speak about the almost sacred quality of the covenant of marriage. That's the real sin we are dealing with. Why don't you tell me more about what Harold said happened?"

"OK. Like I told you, I started screaming at him and called him every name I could think of. He sat there, receiving blow after blow, not even trying to defend himself. It was as if he had called himself all those names before."

"Did he tell you how it happened?"

"Yeah, after I ran out of names to call him and my throat was hoarse from screaming, I finally asked, 'How did this happen?' I'd heard about people repressing their sexual orientation and then suddenly discovering it in some sort of midlife crisis."

"He told me that he was at this conference in San Francisco last year." She paused. "Why doesn't God destroy that city if He's going to destroy one?" Then she continued her narrative. "Anyway, one evening after a meeting, he and another guy went out for some drinks. They didn't realize that the bar they picked attracted a lot of gays. A couple of guys tried to hit on them, and they started kidding each other about who was most attractive." She shook her head. "They were pretty drunk by the time they got back to the hotel. There was a wet bar in the other guy's room, so they continued to drink and kid each other. The way he told it, before they knew it, they were sort of experimenting with each other." She lifted her hand to her throat and her mouth opened as if she were gagging. "It's so disgusting; I don't even want to talk about it. If he's gay, why didn't he admit it before he married me and got me pregnant?"

"Maybe he's not really gay," I said cautiously.

"What do you mean? He fucked a guy, didn't he? He sure wouldn't do that if he were straight, would he?"

"As I understand it, our sexual orientation is on a continuum. There are some people on either extreme, but most people find themselves somewhere along the continuum. It doesn't make you gay because you feel affection for someone of the same sex. Is it possible that your husband had never recognized any attraction to another man before that unfortunate night?"

"That's what he told me. He said he had never, ever, had such thoughts before, and the next morning they were both horrified at what they had done. They made a promise never to tell anyone else. But it kept eating away at him. Then your sermon hits him between the eyes. It was like taking the stopper out of a bottle. He couldn't keep it in any longer. Oh, how I wish we had never gone to church that Sunday." She started keening as if someone precious to her had died.

"It was eating away at his soul, Eleanor. I can't promise you that your relationship will survive this, but I think it is pretty clear, from what you have told me, that if he hadn't told you, he would have continued to spiral down and would probably have killed himself."

She looked at me through her tears. "I . . . I . . . wouldn't have wanted that. He has been a good

fa . . .father and that would have been devastating for the ch . . . children. Oh, pastor, what am I going to tell the children? They know we are having a fight. I made him move out. But they keep thinking that pretty soon it will be better, and he will come back."

"I wish I had an answer for that. I don't. I am willing to work with you, and with Harold if he will let me, in trying to find a solution."

"So you don't think Harold is going to hell because he did that? If he promised to never, ever, ever to do it again, do you think God would save him?"

"We could have a longer discussion sometime about the Bible and homosexuality, but, for now, let me just say that despite our tradition, the Bible is far from clear in the very few passages that even speak about it. In one of those passages, it does suggest it is a sin, but it is a sin that is equivalent to gossip and being greedy. For all our sakes, we better trust that the grace of God is stronger than any of those behaviors.

"The real question that we need to deal with is that the covenant of your marriage has been broken. What would you have done differently if it had been another woman?"

Her eyes glinted as she said, "I would have made him pay big time, but if he was really sorry, we would have worked it through. But that's different. I don't mean to be overly bold, but I know how to compete with other women. I mean, look at me, pastor." She rose, slipped off her suit jacket and presented herself as if she was a model walking down the runway. "You're a man. I'm desirable, don't you think?"

I thought I knew what was happening. I had focused on Eleanor's every word for the past 45 minutes. Such an experience can evoke feelings of intimacy and be easily misinterpreted.

"Eleanor, I think the real issue we should . . ."

"It must be pretty lonely being a pastor. Do you ever look out some Sunday at some of your more attractive members and wonder what it would be like? You don't have to answer that, but I'll just bet some of them are wondering that about you."

"Somehow I doubt that, Eleanor, but we need to . . ."

"Oh, you're wrong. Think about it. If a woman wants to get close to God, you may be the best path available."

I felt uncomfortable. I resisted the impulse to reach up and loosen my collar. I only hoped that my face wasn't turning red. I knew that the traumatic experience with Harold had shattered her self-confidence. In a crazy sort of way, she seemed to be trying to reaffirm her desirability as a woman and confirm Harold's straying was not her fault.

I spoke brusquely. "Eleanor, we're here to discuss what has happened between you and Harold. Your marriage and your children are at risk."

She blinked and her eyes lost their trance-like glaze? "OK, so you are not available. Can you at least tell me that you find me attractive? I really need that right now."

"You are definitely an attractive woman, Eleanor. Harold would really be the loser if he lost you as a mate."

"Thank you. I've heard some other women in this church say it, and now I have experienced it myself. You really know how to listen, and that can feel very good.

"Harold knew how to listen—once. I think that was what first attracted me to him." She snickered. "Just my luck. I meet two men who know how to listen, and one's a friggin faggot, and the other is a preacher with morals."

I tried to offer a stern look. "Eleanor, I have serious questions as to whether Harold is gay, and, even if he is, the word 'faggot' is inappropriate."

She grimaced. "OK, I will be a good girl now and behave myself, but sometimes it feels good to be a little crude in a safe place. I never understood what a sanctuary was before, but you are good at offering sanctuary."

"When was the last time you talked to Harold?"

"We spoke yesterday. He wanted to take the children to lunch."

"How did he sound?"

"Pretty low. It seemed to lift his spirits when I agreed that the children could have Saturday lunch with him. He really is a good father."

"Eleanor, a few minutes ago, you acted in a way that seems out of character."

She blushed. "I'm sorry. I bet you thought you were in a scene from *Desperate Housewives*."

"What I thought was that, for a moment, you were overpowered by an almost uncontrollable need to affirm your worth. I raise that for two reasons. One, I want us to get beyond it. And two, I want to suggest that Harold may be feeling that same sense of unworthiness."

"I think I see what you mean. I've been so angry I haven't given him or his needs much thought."

"Whatever else is true, he is both the father of your children and, up until that incident, had been a supportive husband. It might be helpful for him to hear that from you."

She stared at the floor in silence. After about a minute, she looked up. "I'll call him as soon as I leave here. Is your secretary right next door?"

"Uh, yes she is."

"Would you ask her to come in for a moment?"

Although a little puzzled, I punched the phone's call button and asked Margaret to step into the office.

As Margaret entered, Eleanor stood up and introduced herself. "Margaret, I'm about to give your boss a very affectionate hug for what he's done for me today, and I asked you to come in to protect his reputation."

Eleanor hugged me, and then she was gone, leaving me a little breathless.

"I never knew being a pastor's secretary could be so much fun," Margaret said with an impish smile on her face.

# 8

# A HYPOCRITICAL
# OATH FOR PASTORS

Mark estimated that the breeze made the wind chill hover around thirty-five degrees. But that wasn't what was chilling him. It wasn't even that he was standing five floors up on the roof of the seminary's bell tower gazing down on the startled crowd that had gathered below. What chilled Mark was the sight of Ethan Bakerson, a recent graduate of the seminary, standing on the ledge looking out across the campus. Ethan held a rifle in his hand.

Ethan had fired a couple of shots, but, for now, no one had been hurt.

"It's all a bunch of crap, people." Ethan spoke through a microphone he had cleverly wired into the bell tower speaker. "You're being fed a bunch of bullshit while the seminary steals your money and prepares you for a profession that is disappearing under your noses." The mike was hooked to his collar so that both his hands were free. "Even if you get a job, it doesn't pay squat."

Mark was a forty-eight year-old, slightly pudgy, bespectacled, five-foot-five-five inch pastor. Ten minutes earlier, he had come out of the seminary bookstore with a cup of hot coffee in his hand. He heard the front window of the bookstore shatter from the impact of the first bullet. A couple of shards of glass landed at his feet. Then he heard a shot from the top of the bell tower as another bullet ricocheted off a statue of Jesus gazing out over the seminary campus.

Mark had always thought of himself as a nerdy, somewhat average pastor, never as a hero. He couldn't explain why, but when he saw the shooter standing on the ledge of the bell tower, he dropped his coffee and ran to the tower. Adrenalin carried him up the five flights of steps. He smelled the sweat of his own fear as he eased the door open and stepped out at the top of the tower. He wiped the fog created by the contrast of temperature from his glasses. The concrete floor of the flat roof was rough and gritty from the tracks of many who had sought the view of the campus from its most prominent perch. It was a constant complaint of the custodial staff that visitors left their sandwich wrappings and occasional wine bottles in their wake. There was a three-foot-fencelike ledge surrounding the roof that was probably about eight inches wide.

Fighting to control his breathing, Mark saw Ethan about thirty feet from him, balancing on the ledge of the roof. Ethan was concentrating on the crowd below, waving his rifle back and forth. He had not heard Mark come through the door.

*What in the world am I doing here*, Mark thought, *and what do I do now?*

He recognized Ethan from a class on church government that Mark had taught as an adjunct professor a couple of years back. He remembered the six-foot-two student with the shock of tightly curled, bright red hair as a very vocal idealist in class discussions. Now, a couple of years later, Ethan had gained about forty pounds. His face looked puffy, and his shoulders hunched up as if carrying a great weight.

"Is this your version of posting your ninety-five theses against the church, Ethan?"

Ethan swung his rifle around to face Mark. "What are you doing here, professor?"

"I thought I was coming to the campus for a break from church work, but your rather dramatic statement caught my attention, so

I thought I'd come up and see what you were trying to say." He remembered from watching TV that you were supposed to establish a relationship with the shooter. "By the way, you can call me Mark." He edged towards Ethan as he spoke. He didn't know what he was going to do, but that was the way he remembered it from the movies.

"Stay back, profess . . . or Mark. You're a decent guy, but you've bought into all this malarkey, and I'm fed up with it. It is all a sham. Full of lies."

*Keep him in conversation*, Mark thought. *Surely someone has called the police by now. All I have to do is stall a little longer.*

"Are you talking about the church, the Christian faith, or this seminary that is full of shit?" Mark didn't normally use crude language, but he wanted to sound bold enough to focus Ethan's attention. The sun slipped behind a cloud, and the chill increased significantly. Mark wished he had on a heavier jacket, but he wasn't sure that was what was causing him to shiver.

"How long have you been a minister, Mark, twenty years?"

"Close to twenty-five now," Mark said.

"How'd you do it?" Mark could hear the stress in his voice. "Didn't you ever realize that resurrection is biologically impossible, forgiveness is for wimps who can't win, and all the church is interested in is sucking the money out of gullible members to protect a failing institution?" His speech increased in pace with a manic like quality.

Before Mark could respond, Ethan pointed his rifle toward Mark. "And don't give me all that 'you got to accept this on faith' crap. I don't know whether God exists or not, but I'm sure as hell convinced that if there is a divine force behind all of this reality, He or She either doesn't give a damn, or IT has a cruel streak a mile wide."

*It's strange*, Mark thought, *I must have preached twenty-five Easter sermons, and I never really asked myself whether I was afraid to die. I guess staring down the barrel of a rifle makes faith rather specific.*

"Put down the rifle, Ethan. The police will be here soon. I know you are as angry as hell, but we can still avoid disaster."

"I passed disaster a long time ago, Mark. Today I'll find out if there is life after death, which I doubt. If there is a God, it will stop fucking with me. Before I end it, however, I'm going to give a small part of the world one last chance to hear some truth."

*I'm not sure who is crazier—Ethan for wanting to commit suicide or me for thinking I can stop him.* Two police cars slid to a stop on the campus lawn followed by a fire truck. A uniformed officer with a megaphone stepped out of one car, carefully keeping the car door between him and the speaker on the roof. *I hope they know what they are doing, or somebody is going to get hurt.*

Ethan directed Mark, "Step towards the edge so that they can see you, but not too close to me," as he swung the rifle back towards the crowd below.

*I can't believe all the crazy people down there*, Mark thought. *Do they really think because they are spectators that they can't be shot. In this day and age, some idiot is probably shooting this with his smart phone hoping to get on the 11 O'clock news.*

"You, on the roof," the officer said through the megaphone, "put the rifle down so that we can talk and no one gets hurt."

"See this man here," Ethan pointed to Mark with his rifle as Mark peered over the ledge. "He's my hostage, and his life is in your hands. Just do as I say, and I'm the only one who has to die today."

He turned back to Mark. "Do what I say, and you'll be OK. I don't want to harm anyone except myself, but I want them to listen first."

"Here's the deal, officer. I'm going to say my piece. You won't even have to waste a sniper's bullet. All you'll have to do is clean up the mess after I fall."

Mark felt the rough concrete of the ledge under his sweaty hand as he turned back toward Ethan. He forced his voice to keep a calm tone. "Talk to me, Ethan. What's happened that brought you to such despair?"

"I'll tell you what happened," said Ethan. "I'm forty-thousand dollars in debt from having studied at this seminary that taught me there is a loving God for whom I should devote my life to serving, but, as far as I can tell, this invisible god has gone AWOL." He realized that his voice was carrying down to the crowd below, and he turned to face them.

"You want to know the truth, people?" His voice vibrated with righteous anger. "We work for a church that's collapsing from within because it is so self-serving and full of hypocrisy that no one under thirty will darken its doors." The pitch of his voice raised. "Even the older generation is beginning to abandon it because their beach house offers more comfort on the weekend. They would rather spend their money on pleasure than on sharing with those in need as the Gospel commands."

"So the church is full of hypocrites, and you're going to commit suicide to teach them a lesson. Is that it?" Mark asked. *The irony is, I share some of his anger only I've learned to survive. Maybe I'm the crazy one.*

"Face it, Mark. Don't you feel like a hypocrite, getting up Sunday after Sunday, and telling people that they should love a neighbor who is willing to betray them to make a few more dollars? I'll bet you tell them that they should trust your absentee God—a god who is willing to allow untold innocent children to starve in this world while Christians support governments who waste billions of dollars building weapons to destroy each other."

"You hold God responsible for the evil of humanity?"

"According to our glorious faith, God created humanity." Ethan held up his other hand to stop Mark's response. "Oh, I know, you are going to remind me that God provided us with free will, and we choose to do evil or not on our own." He continued to address both Mark and the crowd below. "Isn't God supposed to be all knowing? Didn't the Almighty One know from the beginning that he was creating a universe in which such cruelty would continue to exist? A child with tinker toys could make a better creation than that." His voice took on a mocking quality. "You pay all that money, and your professors can't even answer a basic question like that. They ought to refund your tuition."

Mark stepped up on the ledge so that both he and Ethan were on the same level. He gave a silent thanks for the Tai Chi course that had improved his sense of balance. Still, it is a long way down.

*I do hope that Ethan is wrong and that there is a God who cares about what is happening.*

"Hey, what are you doing?" Ethan's eyes grew in size. "Get down from there. You could fall."

Ethan moved forward towards Mark. He started to reach out, but then drew back. "Don't come any closer, Mark. I don't want you to get hurt. I just want the world to hear the truth for once."

"You asked me a question, Ethan. The answer is I do feel like a hypocrite, sometimes."

Since Mark didn't have a microphone, the crowd below could only hear what Ethan was saying, scattered words of half a conversation, as they watched two people balanced as on a high-wire on the bell tower ledge.

"I think," Mark continued, "it is one of the unspoken burdens of the ministry. We are not given the luxury of taking a few months off when we are filled with doubts. Rather, we have to stand up each Sunday morning and try to offer hope and courage to a people who are desperate for some good news that will help them survive."

"So you know it's a lie, but you do it anyway." Ethan said. For a moment, he had hesitated, but now he seemed to recover his anger. Again he lifted the rifle moving it between Mark and the crowd below.

"I didn't say it was a lie. I do feel like a hypocrite at times, but I keep acting like a pastor because people need a reason to hope."

"Bullshit, a lie is a lie." Ethan hurled the words like bullets at Mark.

"Just a moment ago, when I stood up on the ledge and you thought I might fall, you almost stopped what you were doing and tried to reach out to keep me from falling." Mark leaned in as if he could push his words into Ethan's ears. "Both of us have our doubts, but we also want to keep others from falling."

"Why do you keep doing it, Mark? Most of your own people don't believe half of what you preach. At least they don't show it in their lives."

"Don't you think I know that, Ethan. They don't believe all of it, but they want to believe it. In a way, they and we are like Jacob."

"Jacob? Jacob who? What are you talking about?"

"Jacob in the Bible," Mark said. "Don't you remember, he was the con artist of con artists?"

The crowd below, in their eagerness to see what was happening, had slowly gathered behind the police cars parked on the quad. Ethan turned to gaze at them. "You see how crazy this faith of yours is?" Ethan shouted to the people below. "I'm holding a rifle five-stories up getting ready to shoot people or jump, and this loony-tunes preacher wants to talk about some obscure character in the Bible."

*Is it progress that he is now mad at me rather than God?* "All right, Ethan. Here's the choice. You can jump and end it now, or we can wrestle with the truth and see if we can find a reason to live."

Ethan stared at Mark for several seconds. "OK, I'll play your game. Jacob, wasn't he that fool that wrestled with God or something like that?"

"That's the one. When I'm feeling most hypocritical, he's my hero."

"The crowd's getting restless, professor. You have five-minutes to convince me, or I'm going to finish this off."

Mark began to talk more rapidly. "As I said, Jacob was a schemer who was willing to take advantage of family and neighbor to get ahead. He was like your worst church member and your most hypocritical pastor bundled together. In him you could see why the evils of the world prosper."

"That just proves my point. Religion has been a con game from the beginning."

"Think about the reason behind all religions," Mark said.

"They are all just a bunch of lies to keep the masses pacified," responded Ethan.

Refusing to take the bait, Mark continued. "All religions seek to answer the question of whether the universe and our lives are just a bunch of accidents or whether there is purpose and meaning to what is happening."

"Shit happens," said Ethan. "There is no truth or purpose."

"Unless God is real and cares for a purpose."

"God is like that lifeless statue of Jesus I shot a few minutes ago," said Ethan. "He or It is irrelevant to what happens here."

"If you're right, then you might as well jump. It doesn't make any difference anyhow. But Jacob challenged God. He grabbed a hold of God and refused to let go until God would bless him or make sense out of life."

While before Ethan was scanning the crowd as he listened, now he focused on Mark. "I don't get it."

*Damn, I think he's actually listening.* Mark edged a little closer. "Jacob, the schemer, is renamed Israel, the one who wrestles with God until the universe makes sense. Israel, his descendents, and the church refuse to accept that what you see is all that there is. We inherit that faith, Ethan. We insist on believing that this universe is going somewhere and our lives have more meaning than just an accident."

"But you can't prove that. I don't even think you believe that."

"Not all the time. No one does. Life gets overwhelming at times. All good pastors are hypocrites. When life gets rough and the questions are without answers, they playact as if it is true until people can believe again. That's what it means to be a hypocrite—to playact at the truth."

"Nice try, Mark, but I can't hold on to God any longer. It just doesn't make sense."

The screech of a police bullhorn interrupted their conversation. "OK, buddy, this has gone on long enough. It's time for you to come down from there."

"OK, copper. You're going to get your wish. We're going to finish this. Did you ever see suicide by cop, Mark? You're about to."

Ethan turned toward the crowd and raised his rifle to firing position. "Die, Jesus!" he shouted and fired at the statue of Jesus in the quadrangle.

Mark saw the red spot from a SWAT team rifle begin to center in on Ethan. "No," he shouted, as he moved toward Ethan. He hoped the SWAT team would hold their fire, and he could push Ethan back onto the rooftop.

As he lunged toward Ethan, his foot slipped. His momentum carried him forward, pushing at Ethan but spinning his body into the air. He knew he was falling, but he wasn't prepared for the sensation of a hot fire entering his upper body. He heard the crowd screaming.

*Nice exit*, he thought. *I wonder if this faith is true or not. Guess it's up to you now, God. Might be a good time for you to intervene.*

Though he had no real awareness of time passing, it was three days later that Mark felt a slight itch behind his eyes. Then he heard the hushed mumbling of other humans. He tried to move his body, an arm, a leg, even a finger and realized that nothing would respond to his intentions. If he could just blink, maybe the itch behind his eyes would go away.

He focused on his eyes. If I can just move an eye, he thought, then I would know that I'm not dead. After what seemed a long time and a lot of energy, slowly one eyelid began to move slightly.

He heard a squeal of delight. "He's coming around. Look, his eye is moving."

As others would explain to him in the next several months of recovery, his body bounced off three church banners on the way down and then into a survivor's net that the firefighters had constructed just in time. The Swat team bullet had ripped through his shoulder, but the wound was healing nicely.

Several days after he awoke, he asked about Ethan. After he was arraigned, a friend explained, Ethan convinced the court that he wasn't a threat, and he was released on a bail raised by contributions from the student body and Mark's own congregation. He came directly to the hospital and refused to leave until he could talk to Mark. When Ethan walked in, his first words were, "Hey, Jacob, I'm so glad you taught me the truth."

"Falling five floors and surviving convinced you?" Mark asked.

"No, risking everything for my sake convinced me. I'll still have my doubts, but you reflected the God I want to believe in. If I had fallen, my life would have ended without value. I was totally focused on myself. If you had fallen to your death, your life would still have had value, not only to me but to those who witnessed what you did and those who told the story to others."

"So are you willing to be a hypocrite with me?" asked Mark.

"I can't think of a more meaningful way to live my life," responded Ethan.

# 9

## A GRIEF OBSERVED

*(Please forgive the scatological language.)*

I can't tell you anything that happens from the time I leave the church, where I'm pastor, until the time I arrive home. My thoughts jump around like water bouncing off a hot skillet. I'd make a person with ADD look like a model of focus. I come back to earth when my Volkswagen suddenly tips up as I run over the curb turning into my driveway. *Way to go, Alan, you dumb shit. Lucky that none of your neighbors are out for an evening stroll.*

I'm not exactly tall, about five-foot-five-inches, but manage to bang my head on the doorframe of the car as I exit. My fury increases when I stumble going up my front steps. You'd think I'm drunk, but I rarely drink anything but a glass of wine and haven't had that today. I take out my key ring, and, naturally, my first choice is the wrong key. If I had any hair left on my head, I'd pull it out. To top it off, the door isn't even locked, but I restrain myself from hitting it with my fist and walk into my house.

Marcia, my wife, places a marker in the book she is reading and stands as I enter the den. She doesn't even have a chance to say hello before acid begins to flow from my mouth.

"Those fucking idiots on the Worship Committee spent two hours arguing about whether the periods of silence I've introduced in the worship service make people too uncomfortable."

"A real stinker of a day, huh?" Marcia says, then turns and puts down the book that she was reading. She has become an expert at knowing that there is a time to speak and a time to refrain from speaking.

"Oh, no," I say as I fling my briefcase across the room, barely missing a flower vase. "It was a perfect day. I consider it one of the privileges of my life to feed the egos of a bunch of self-indulgent prima donnas. Those fucking morons couldn't distinguish an ethical value from a Krispy Kreme donut."

Marcia raises one eyebrow but remains silent.

In one corner of my fevered brain, I recognize how lucky I am that this wonderful woman agreed to marry me. I know many other guys made their play for this five-foot-three-inch, slim, auburn haired, vivacious woman who is standing before me. For reasons I don't understand, she chose to marry a short, bald, pudgy clergy whose salary can barely keep us above the poverty level.

That part of my brain, however, is in recess while the reptilian part has chosen fight over flight even if the enemy is not present. "Do you know what that God damned son of a bitch Reginald Fiedler said at the budget meeting this afternoon? This prick had the fucking nerve to suggest that the church couldn't afford to give the pastor a raise since the membership had not increased enough even to pay for critical building repairs. It never occurred to any of them that their cliquish, tight-assed behavior might be one of the reasons that no one wants to join the church."

Marcia stands there looking at me.

I rarely swear and never include God or Jesus in such a vain way. A small echo of conscience rises to the surface. "I'm sorry, Marcia. I don't mean to offend you."

"I'm not offended. Before I met you, I dated guys who couldn't say a dozen words without naming God, Jesus, and various bodily functions. It's just that this is so unlike you."

"Well, maybe I ought to change. Christ Almighty, I'm sick and tired of exhausting myself trying to please these self-centered pissants who don't give a shit what God wants or what it means to be a faithful church."

"You once told me that it was God you were serving."

"Yeah, that was one of my delusions. In case you haven't noticed, it's the megachurch over on State Street that seems to be reaping all of God's blessings lately."

She doesn't say a word or show any signs of disapproval. She just continues to listen to my ranting. I don't seem able to stop.

"If God exists, and the jury is still out on that, I don't see one fucking bit of evidence that He—and you're right it probably is one more Neanderthal male—I don't see one shitty sliver of evidence that God or anyone else cares what I do. If I died tomorrow, who in the hell would care?"

We have been standing about six feet apart, though I've been shouting as if we were in separate rooms. Marcia tilts her head slightly, closes the gap between us, and as she enfolds me in her arms she says the two sweetest words in the universe.

"I care."

I finally shut up.

Then the strangest thing begins to happen. I feel the room begin to shake. We have never had an earthquake in this section of the country. Then I realize that it is not the house that is shaking.

My body is shaking, and I am sobbing.

After a few minutes, I begin to regain some control. "I'm sorry," I say. "If I need proof of God's love for me, I only have to recognize that God has given you to me."

"I feel the same way about eight-five percent of the time," she says.

At first, I feel my insecurity rise up. Then I feel my wife's body shake as she continues to hold me but giggles as well.

I relax as she steps back.

She looks at me for a second. "Alan, I want you to sit down and cooperate with what I'm about to do."

"Right here in the living room," I say with a smirk on my face.

"Maybe later tonight, lover boy, but right now I have another idea."
She takes out her Smart phone.

"Who are you calling?" I ask. I don't want anyone else to know about my imbecilic behavior.

"Just sit," she says. "I'll get you a glass of wine, but I also want to ask Phyllis to come over."

Phyllis, my wife's good friend, is a psychologist.

I start to object, but Marcia is already on the phone.

"Phyllis, it's Marcia. You know what we were talking about yesterday?" She pauses and listens. "You were right, and I need you to come over right now. Don't bother to knock, just come on in."

She clicks off, heads to the kitchen, and returns with a glass of wine.

"Marcia, I know Phyllis is a very smart woman, but I am embarrassed enough about my behavior. I don't want . . ."

"Hush! I've seen this build up in you over the last couple of years. I'm not about to sit by and let you be torn apart anymore without fighting back."

"I'm just tired, that's all. I promise I'll take some extra time off and get some rest. What do you mean, you've seen it build up—what's built up?"

"Phyllis calls it secondary grief. Just hear her out, Alan."

Before I can respond, in walks our neighbor. Phyllis is a large woman, just under six feet I'd guess. She has an ageless quality, but I'd guess she is approaching sixty. I've never seen her when she wasn't dressed professionally, but tonight she has on a blue sweat suit with a maize wolverine on it.

She sees me glance at the insignia and blushes slightly. "It's a gift from my granddaughter. She knows it drives her loyal UNC grandpa crazy."

"I've just never seen you in anything but a business suit."

"It's an authority thing," she says and smiles.

"Marcia says you two have been talking about something to do with grief," I say.

"Alan, I know that you have been a good pastor at this congregation for several years. During that time, I imagine, you've helped a number of people through periods of grief.

"Yeah," I say, but I'm sure my face shows the hesitancy I feel. "I'm not sure what that has to do with me."

"Let's not start with you. Let's start with what you know about grief that makes you a good pastor," Phyllis says. "For example, I'm sure you can list the normal stages of grief that people pass through?"

"I think the classic ones are denial, anger, bargaining, and hopefully acceptance. It's somewhat similar to the stages people go through when facing death." I don't know where this is going, but I feel myself relaxing a little as we start talking about an area with which I am very familiar.

"And when a person experiences deep grief," Phyllis continues, "what are some of the effects on that person both physically and emotionally?"

"Physically it makes the person's body more vulnerable to breakdown, and they lack energy," I say.

"And emotionally," she presses.

"I'm not sure what the studies show," I say, "but from my experience, people in grief become more isolated They lose perspective as well as emotional control. Their pain is so great that they are almost entirely self-absorbed."

"I agree, Alan. Some of my grief-frozen patients lose all awareness of their impact on others."

"Wait a minute," I say, suddenly being aware of where this conversation is going, "I am not grieving. I'll admit that I have been working too hard, and, yes, I did lose some emotional control this evening, but it is nothing that a couple of good nights' sleep and maybe an extra day of vacation won't cure."

Marcia comes over and sits beside me, squeezing my leg gently. "Alan, Phyllis has been doing some research on what she calls secondary grief that surgeons experience in their practice. The other day she and I were discussing some parallels in the ministry."

"OK, OK," I say, holding up my hands in a sign of surrender. "If you'll join us in a glass of wine, I'll play along. Lord knows after frightening the hell out of my wife when I came home tonight, I owe her that much."

Marcia bounces up and heads to the kitchen for the bottle of wine and two more glasses. "I'll also get some cheese while you two begin," she says.

Her shoulders are less bunched up as if she feels relief that this conversation is happening.

"So tell me about your research," I say.

"One day over at the hospital, I opened a wrong door by accident and found one of the hospital's best surgeons weeping in the closet. He had just lost a little girl in surgery. Like the compassionate person he was, he had sat with the family for over an hour absorbing their pain. Then he left them with the chaplain. No one noticed him entering the closet."

"I guess people are so focused on the family of the person who has died that they never think about the impact on the medical staff," I say.

"I began to do some research," Phyllis says. "I picked out five surgeons and a few other doctors or excellent nurses in the critical care areas. I got the hospital's permission to question support staff and administrators who were close to these people."

Several years ago, a friend clued me in to the importance of paying attention to the doctors at the time of death. "Sounds like some worthwhile research," I say.

"Marcia tells me that you had a rather traumatic death in the congregation last month," Phyllis says.

"I was telling her about young Eric Singer who was killed in the motorcycle accident," Marcia says.

"Yeah, the whole congregation was torn apart over that one," I say. "Maybe you're right. That really took it out of me, too. He was a wonderful kid. I'll give myself some extra time to get restored."

"That's good," Phyllis says, "but let me take this a step further."

"What do you mean?" I ask.

"From what Marcia says, you are pretty good at helping people in your congregation work through difficult emotional times."

"It's a necessary part of our profession," I say.

"So tell me, Alan, what specifically did you do to help the Singer family and the congregation face their grief."

"Nothing really unusual," I say, "just good pastoral practice. I spent a lot of time with the various members of the family, both individually and as a group."

"What did you do when you were with them?" Phyllis asks.

"Mostly just listened. When people are in deep grief, they feel as if their lives are in chaos. All the familiar structures that used to give them a sense of security have vanished. You understand this. Mostly you encourage them to tell stories, including hopefully some fun ones, to remind them of the good memories that they share. Words help us give form to our feelings and bring some order to our chaos."

"And for the congregation?" Phyllis presses.

"Congregations always feel helpless at such times. Deep pain scares all of us, yet most people don't know how to respond.

Sometimes they even try to explain why the tragedy happened, which isn't helpful to the family at all."

"Al was at his best during that time," Marcia says with pride in her voice. "He told the congregation about the importance of sending personal notes rather than preprinted cards or emails. Under his guidance, I think the congregation responded wonderfully."

"Who sent personal notes to you, Al?" Phyllis asks.

"I didn't lose a child," I say, feeling irritation rising in me. "My focus was the Singer family and, secondarily, the congregation to work through their grief. People go a little crazy in times of grief. They all needed some help."

"But you were above it all, as if in a little balloon where feelings couldn't penetrate." Phyllis says.

"I didn't say that. It's just that there wasn't time to pay attention to my needs. In addition to the funeral and being present to them, I had a Sunday service coming up, a budget meeting to prepare for, two baptisms, and a newsletter to get out. I think I also had to speak to the custodian about some member's complaint about cleanup. "

"Why didn't you tell the Singers to just suck it up and get on with life?" Phyllis asks.

That really irritates me. *What type of psychologist is she anyway?* "Is that some type of sick joke? Next you're going to spout crap like 'Time heals all wounds' or 'God wanted another flower in his garden.' That's the type of shit that fries my ass."

Phyllis doesn't seem bothered by my reaction. She waits until I run down and then says, "But isn't that what you were telling yourself to do? Marcia tells me that you were very close to the Singer boy. Surely you felt deep pain, but no one offered you comfort, did they? You wouldn't even give yourself permission to acknowledge your own pain. You just sucked it up and kept going."

Marcia reaches over and refills both of our glasses. "Why don't you share that checklist you were using with the doctors?" she says to Phyllis.

I'm still trying to decide whether I want to hit Phyllis or stomp out of the room in a huff. She clearly doesn't understand the nature of ministry.

Phyllis pulls a small notebook out of her pocket. "It's just a partial list of some of the changes that the support staff noticed about the doctors and nurses in the critical care area when they lost a patient that they had grown close to."

Phyllis begins to read from her notes: "They seemed to withdraw from casual conversation, as if they couldn't be bothered. Others would say that they appeared more weighed down by life. They made cynical remarks about the hospital, the medical profession, and life in general. There was a loss of a sense of humor, and they seemed less tolerant of even the littlest mistakes by others."

"Does any of that sound familiar?" Marcia asks.

"Look, I appreciate your concern," I say, "and some of those characteristics are accurate, but they are also true about people who are just overworked. As Sigmund Freud said, 'Sometimes a cigar is just a cigar.'" I pause and take a sip of wine. Actually I take a gulp of wine.

"If it was just this one tragic accident," Phyllis says, "I wouldn't press the issue. But Alan, I've talked enough with Marcia to know that there are many areas of grief that you experience in the ministry. What I want to suggest to you is that they are cumulative. "

"I understand what you are saying, but what you don't understand is that's just the way it is in the ministry," I say.

"I don't doubt that," says Phyllis. "The question is how does a good pastor handle his or her grief without getting locked in to denial and, like many doctors, building shields around themselves for protection.

I look at both of them. They don't say a word. The silence hangs there.

I stand up. "Grief, huh, I think what you are suggesting is that the better a pastor is, the more pain they absorb."

"That's the way I see it," says Phyllis.

"Helping people work through their grief is one of your great gifts, Alan," Marcia says. "I just want you to apply those same gifts to yourself."

I walk over to where my briefcase landed and straighten up the vase that sits precariously on its stand. "For the sake of my wife and this house, I guess I'd better try."

I guess how I do that is another story for another time

# 10

## GOD'S CHURCH

When we sense a call from God to enter the ministry, and even as we study the critical tools of biblical and theological truths that are part of our faith, for many of us there is a sense of awe that we have been called.

In the last several decades, the sense of call has been downplayed because it seemed to many that we were claiming that we were somehow better than others. In many ways, we struggle with the assumption of arrogance attributed to Israel that they countered by saying that it was not that Israel was better, but the miracle was that God took a no people and made them God's people and that reflects the awe of our calling 1 Peter 2:10.

It is not because of any quality in our lives but because of the mysterious choice of God that we have been touched for this special calling. To be called by God for the pastoral ministry (and there are many other calls to which God can call us) is to be spoken to by a voice from beyond time and space to serve a people who also are called by God for a particular ministry in our world.

A major cause of stress for a pastor is the disconnect between the ideals of faith shaped by his or her beliefs and the pressures and demands of serving a church. A pastor is called by God and hired by a congregation. Sometimes, these two forces are in tension.

With all of the facets of ministry, it is easy to be overwhelmed by the demands of the profession and lose touch with the source of our call. The necessary mundane nature of many of the demands of ministry can also blur the special nature of this body, the Body of Christ, chosen to incarnate God's expression of truth.

The good news is that God is neither dependent on our purity nor defeated by the acts of faithlessness of clergy or congregation. Ministry is a complex mosaic of strengths and weaknesses in a confusing and sin-filled world. According to theologian Shirley Guthrie,

> *The church is the only 'club' in the world that accepts as members only those who are not qualified to belong to it!*
> *(Christian Doctrine, page 357)*

Ministers are strong and weak, faithful and faithless, as are the members of their congregations. Each week clergy gather with their congregation to hear the Scripture, sing the songs, and pray the prayers that remind them that there is more to life than meets the eye. When we are honest in our confession of sins, we discover that our hope rests in a power beyond ourselves, and there is reason for hope. The miracle of the church is not in our faithfulness but in God's faithfulness. We are witnesses to how our confused reality keeps being interrupted by grace.

Clergy stand in the breach between God and humanity. We, too, are imperfect, but we have been called by God. Like Moses in leading the Israelites out of Egypt, we find ourselves speaking to the people on behalf of God and also turning to beg for God's mercy on behalf of the people. We often feel like neither audience is listening, but we are not free to abandon our call.

When one seeks to understand the nature of ministry, it is important to recognize that not all stress comes from negative experiences. The ministry is filled with very positive and affirming interactions that cause a pastor to feel awed that s/he is privileged to be a part of them. Even positive experiences place a drain on one's emotional reserves.

High octane experiences, both negative and positive, frequently tumble on top of each other in the ministry. They are interspersed with many mundane, even tedious demands of the profession that take their toll in a different form. There is a particular danger of moving from an adrenaline-pumping event in one moment to a mind-numbing meeting that solves nothing the next moment. Mix that with listening to how someone has taken offense at something you did, or the heart-breaking experience of watching a friend's marriage disintegrate, or the pain of strangers who have come to you in desperate need for help and you have a sense of the daily encounters in the ministry.

At its most boring, there is something special about the ministry and frequently it is a full-time, hair-raising adventure that is anything but boring. Many clergy fail to recognize the critical need to return to the well frequently for refreshment. This book seeks to provide parabolic stories of the complexity of ministry as a supplement to *A Company of Pastors* which offers an opportunity to build a support group of clergy.

Please give serious consideration to taking time to focus on your spiritual health. In *A Company of Pastors*, I have provided a design for your personal spiritual retreat. Choosing to take a day to care for your own spirit can have significant personal benefits. Deliberately focusing on listening to God's call can strengthen your ministry and life.

You are also invited to go to the Presbytery Pastoral Care Network (PPCN) *www.pastoralcarenetwork.org* for additional resources that can support the ministry of the church. In addition, you can subscribe to my blog *www.smccutchan.com* where I provide weekly suggestions about how to nurture the health of clergy and the church. While the PPCN was initiated by Presbyterians, it is open to all who love the church.

We benefit from your support, but these resources are available at no cost.

Join in my campaign to "build respect for clergy one story at a time."

# 11

## ABOUT THE AUTHOR

 Steve spent thirty-eight years in the pastoral ministry interpreting the Gospel to lay people who experience the tension of division in their world. For twenty-three years, he combined ministry with his middle-class congregation with monthly involvement in counseling the poor in his city. He helped found the *Presbyterian Inter-Racial Dialogue* that in November 2012 celebrated twenty years working with six Presbyterian churches, three predominantly black and three predominantly white, building community that breaks down the barriers of racism. The story of that experience is told in *Let's Have Lunch* available on Amazon.

Since retirement in 2006, he has focused on developing resources to assist in the care of clergy. He leads webinars on both writing and the care of clergy and edits the Newsletter for the Presbytery Pastoral Care Network, *www.pastoralcarenetwork.org*

He blogs regularly on various aspects of the support of clergy, www.smccutchan.com

In addition to these short stories, he has published a mystery novel *A Star and a Tear* that explores the symbiotic relationship between sexuality and spirituality. His purpose in his fiction writings is *to build respect for clergy one story at a time.* All of his books are available on Amazon amzn.to/13VO446.

If you enjoyed this book or any of his other publications, it will be very helpful if you would go to that site amzn.to/13VO446 and write a review of the books that you have read.

If you have enjoyed these tales, it would be helpful if you would go to amzn.to/13VO446 and write a review.

# 12

## RESOURCES BY STEPHEN McCUTCHAN

*www.smccutchan.com*

### HEALTHY CLERGY MAKE HEALTHY CONGREGATIONS

| | |
|---|---|
| *A Company of Pastors:* | Amazon |
| *Clergy Tales—Tails* (3 Volumes) | Amazon |
| *A Star & A Tear (mystery novel)* | Amazon |
| *An Interim Pastor's Gift* | Amazon |
| *God Laughs—Why Don't You?* | Amazon |

### THE WATER SERIES
(A devotional series based on the Revised *Common Lectionary*)

| | | |
|---|---|---|
| *Water From the Well* | (YearA) | CSS pub |
| *Streams of Living Water* | (Year B) | CSS pub |
| *Water From the Rock* | (Year C) | CSS pub |

## BIBLICAL RESOURCES

*Experiencing the Psalms*        Smyth & Helwys

*Good News for a Fractured Society*      Author House

## CDs DESIGNED FOR SUPPORT OF PASTORS

*A Deep Well for the Pastor*       www.smccutchan.com

*Laughter From the Well*         www.cdbaby.com

## COMMUNITY ISSUES

*Let's Have Lunch*          Amazon

www.ingramcontent.com/pod-product-compliance
Lightning Source LLC
Chambersburg PA
CBHW020324130626
46549CB00003B/999